IN THEIR OWN WORDS

"Seeing that I please a woman, sexually and otherwise, is the biggest turn-on of all."

"Just a little kiss, sincere and impassioned, can stir a man's heart more than hours of lovemaking."

"The most arousing words to me are simply—'I love you.'"

"Why aren't women more aware of the power they have over men?"

What do men really want? Here are just a few of the heartfelt responses from the more than 5,000 men surveyed in this provocative book. What finally emerges is the startling truth about how they feel about love, sex, and relationships— an insightful guide for every woman who wants to understand her man.

---

BRIGITTE NIOCHE, a former model and dress designer, runs Total Image Plus, a service that offers women advice on wardrobe planning. She is the author of *The Sensual Dresser*.

# WHAT
# TURNS
# MEN ON

## BRIGITTE NIOCHE

A SIGNET BOOK

NEW AMERICAN LIBRARY

A DIVISION OF PENGUIN BOOKS USA INC.

NAL BOOKS ARE AVAILABLE AT QUANTITY DISCOUNTS WHEN USED
TO PROMOTE PRODUCTS OR SERVICES. FOR INFORMATION PLEASE
WRITE TO PREMIUM MARKETING DIVISION, NEW AMERICAN LIBRARY,
1633 BROADWAY, NEW YORK, NEW YORK 10019.

SIGNET, SIGNET CLASSIC, MENTOR, ONYX, PLUME, MERIDIAN
and NAL BOOKS are published by New American Library,
a division of Penguin Books U.S.A. Inc.,
1633 Broadway, New York, New York 10019

First Printing, July, 1989

1   2   3   4   5   6   7   8   9

PRINTED IN THE UNITED STATES OF AMERICA

For every woman who loves
herself, men, and life—
and for the men I love

# CONTENTS

# PREFACE

The purpose of this book is to share with you the thoughts and feelings of over five thousand men from all walks of life—married and single, of different ages and professions, from all over the country.

By listening to what they have to say, you'll find out how they think relationships between men and women can be satisfying and long-lasting even in this era of change. Their statements convey their overwhelming desire and craving to please their woman, sexually as well as otherwise, and show how relationships and marriages depend on the little things of everyday life.

This book is the result of a nationwide survey conducted over a two-year period. All replies were sent anonymously. Only age, profession, marital status, and location were revealed, making the answers honestly reflect the men's feelings and experiences.

Their suggestions and advice will help women to open up new ways of communication that will make for more satisfying relationships, happier marriages, and better lives. They will also be useful in finding a man. Knowing what a man expects and knowing how to handle a situation is half the battle—and you will see how important good negotiation skills are. You will discover many different sides and characteristics of men, including some you never suspected.

As with my earlier book, *The Sensual Dresser*, I am unable to name but thank all the people who helped me complete this project and who never stopped encouraging me to continue. I would especially like to thank the 5,289 men who participated in this survey. Their openness and enthusiasm was evident at all times, making this information invaluable. They also proved that many so-called clichés that originated a long time ago are still true today.

To these men I express not only my own appreciation, but that of every woman who will read this book.

The following letter shows us how most men felt about answering this survey:

> **Thank you for allowing me to get these feelings out in the open and off my back. Even though these re-**

sponses are anonymous, it's a good way to release pent-up feelings.

I hope that I've not been too vulgar in my answers, but they are honest and best describe my emotions. I've told no one most of these things, and it's been fun to get them out, as well as a relief. These are things one never writes down, so it's something like therapy.

Sincerely,
A women-lover living in Milwaukee

## CHAPTER ONE

# Choosing a Man

According to the result of this survey, men feel that women should be more discriminating and demanding than they are. They should say what they want, sexually as well as otherwise, and they should never make compromises that are unreasonable or unacceptable to them.

The testimonies make it clear that most men want to make their woman happy. They are not interested in someone who only wants to please them. In their opinion, happiness, and often sexual excitement, comes from giving pleasure to the one you love. Pleasing a woman in all areas of life and seeing how much she enjoys it confirms the male ego—an opportunity many women miss by not saying what they want and like. This is especially sad when we think of what women have to offer. Let us take a look and see what exactly that is. Ourselves, our bodies and our love, our understanding and support, all that we possess. In return we should ask and receive the respect and love of our partner.

The experience of one of the respondents illustrates this point well:

> I fell head over heels in love with Marion the first time we met. We saw each other every day and spent nearly a year together. She was a good lover and I admired her good looks. Yet she started to irritate me by never asking for anything. Her response to my questions about what she wanted and liked was always: "Darling, whatever you want is fine with me." When finally I told her that it was over between us, she broke down and said: "What did I do wrong? I gave you everything—myself, my life, my thoughts—and I never asked for anything. All I wanted was to please you!" She never gave me the satisfaction of pleasing her, which made me feel very inadequate in the long run, and took the excitement out of the relationship.

Today men want neither a submissive nor a dominating woman; they want to respect their woman and please her. A doctor from Michigan put it this way: **"I want to put**

**women on pedestals and love them."** It would certainly be a great loss for any woman if she missed finding her pedestal because she didn't let the right man put her up there—and according to this survey, there is one out there for every woman alive.

How do you find the right man? By being aware of your femininity, by knowing what you want, by understanding yourself, and by using these assets discriminately. A musician from Phoenix said: **"I think men now are more than ever ready to accept their partner on an equal and mutually satisfying level. It's up to the woman to know herself and let us know what she wants."**

### Be Confident

**"The most important characteristic in making a woman sensual and attractive is confidence. A confident woman believes in herself and enjoys herself, not only sexually but in anything she does,"** wrote a computer programmer from Michigan.

This is certainly true, but unfortunately not every woman has confidence. What is it? Where does it come from? It is not necessarily a characteristic of good-looking, successful people—in fact, they often have problems with insecurity. Confidence is the result of self-esteem. A woman who has accepted herself for what she is will find this peace of mind. It will

15

make her agreeable, pleasant, and likable—
and therefore happy and confident.

What do men want? Let's look at one question asked in the survey: Which characteristic stimulates you the most?

| | |
|---|---|
| Assertiveness | 64% |
| Helplessness | 17% |
| Shyness | 16% |
| Vulgarity | 3% |

To cultivate your confidence, don't look to others for guidelines. For example, don't compare your love life with that of others and try to compete. It might depress you to know that someone else has three orgasms when you have only one. If one is enough for you, you're not worse than that other person, just different.

Or if you read that other women go to bed with a man on their first date, don't feel compelled to do the same thing if you don't want to. Being confident is being yourself. If you're not, you will project a distorted image of yourself, which will make you insecure. How long can you pretend? Remember that the people who really love you, love you for what you are, not for the outer self you present.

**"I find assertiveness stimulating and refreshing. In my studies of communications and my experience with the opposite sex,**

I've found that aggressive or non-assertive persons either want to dominate me or be dominated. I believe a relationship should be interdependent." That is the opinion of a man involved in human resource development. And a senior music major from Minneapolis said: "The ideal woman has self-confidence and is independent. I would like to feel that she doesn't need me, but wants me anyway. For me, two people exist independently and fulfill each other intimately, emotionally, and spiritually."

*Take Responsibility for What You Want*

Because of society's ideas about what's "nice" and what "isn't," many women miss out on what they really want. The only way some of us escape this trap is when things develop in such a way that they "just happen." Let me explain: I'm sure that in almost every woman's life there was at least one man whom she wanted and could have had if she had made a move. She didn't dare because it wasn't a "nice" thing to do. But if the two of them had been stuck alone in a rainstorm somewhere, what happened wouldn't have been her fault—it "just happened!"

Anne visits her parents, who live in the country, about once a month. During her last visit she was introduced to a young man who had just opened a restaurant in their little town. She liked him the moment she saw

17

him, and more than that, she felt a strong physical attraction. This was something she had always had trouble admitting to herself, because in her mind it was not an emotion women gave into. When her mother suggested they have dinner in the new restaurant, she pretended to have a headache and no appetite. Not aware that her daughter had already met the new owner, the mother tried to change her mind by saying, "Come along anyway, then you can meet the young man who now owns the place. He is very attractive, you'll see!"

That was just what Anne was afraid of, so instead of taking responsibility for her feelings, she stayed at home and had a boring evening.

On her way to town the next day, her car broke down. She was already late and this was really messing things up. Annoyed, she looked around, wondering what to do, when suddenly a Jeep came down the road. When the car stopped and the driver leaned out to ask if he could help, she saw that it was the young man from the restaurant. After looking at her car and seeing that there was nothing he could do to make it go, he offered her a lift. During their conversation he said, "Since you are already late and you have to wait for the tow truck, what about dinner?"

She accepted. He had given her enough reasons why she could accept without compromising her feelings, without looking anxious, without taking responsibility for what might happen.

Unfortunately, these accidents occur more often in the world of fictional romance than in our own. We have to face the fact that sometimes we want to do things that are, according to our own or society's standards, inappropriate. Who benefits from our conventional behavior? Most of the time no one does. Instead, our lack of courage to break these standards prevents us from doing what we really want to do.

A young pharmacist gave this advice: **"In my opinion, women would enjoy life more if they admitted to themselves that they do want and enjoy men, and go after them."**

*Project the Right Signals*

A realistic woman knows that meeting a man cannot be left to chance. She knows that she has to do her part, and her part is to communicate that she is available. **"Some women are so standoffish that even if they were twice as beautiful as they are, I wouldn't be interested in meeting them,"** commented a sales representative from Los Angeles.

Perhaps the women he was referring to weren't looking, but if you are, check your attitude. Don't come across as haughty or indifferent, and don't wait for someone to twist your arm. Keep your options open by being aware of the men around you, and allow them to be aware of you.

A lot is said and written about places where one can meet a man—museums, racecourses, conventions, singles bars, classes, and so on. But the idea of going anyplace with the specific purpose of finding a man is depressing, if not degrading, for many women. Having to go out on the prowl because no one is showing an interest in you is not good for your self-esteem either, but this can be avoided by projecting the right signals. These signals can also overcome a lot of obstacles, as we hear from this man:

> I know a woman who is neither beautiful nor young, but rather plain and on the heavy side. She has never had trouble meeting men. She didn't throw herself at their feet or jump into bed with just anyone. What she has is an open and friendly attitude that communicates her interest in the opposite sex. Since men find these qualities attractive, she had no problem finding a man to have a lasting and serious relationship with. As a matter of fact, she married a good-looking man fifteen years younger than she.

We won't go further into where to meet men because, as this thirty-year-old accountant from Pennsylvania tells us quite rightly: **"If a woman gives off the right signals and keeps an open mind toward men, anyplace is a good place. There are men everywhere, and they are not all married."**

*Encourage a Man to Approach You*

When *you* see a man you like, who really turns you on, it's up to you to go a step further and encourage him to come closer. The old cliché that "a man chases a woman until she catches him" is still true.

When you see him across the room, let your eyes look into his for a moment. The next time you look over, give him a smile, and another, and another. He'll get the message. Don't be afraid of rejection. Showing that you are ready and willing is where taking responsibility for a relationship starts. If you still doubt whether he'll respond to your encouragement, remember that a willing woman is one of the hardest things for a man to resist.

If you're out with one or more women, keep in mind that most men will not dare to approach a group of women. Since many men fear rejection by a woman, they won't take the risk of being rejected in front of a group. If you are really attracted to someone and don't want to lose out on an opportunity, find a reason to pass him, thereby giving him a chance to speak to you. You may also encourage a man to approach you if you're alone somewhere, not with the idea of finding Mr. Right, but enjoying lunch in a pleasant restaurant, taking a walk, or sipping a glass of wine in a bar (not a singles bar).

You may be asking why the woman has to make the first step. There are several answers. The first and most important one is because *you* want something. You want to meet a man, you want a relationship, you want to be happy. Unfortunately, when emotions come into play we lose our objectivity. What can you get in life without having to do something first? Nothing! So instead of being disturbed because you have to take action, don't overlook the fact that doing so puts you in the driver's seat.

Second, there are many shy men out there. Your reaching out will help them overcome their shyness. It will also tell them something about your personality. Here are some comments on the subject of a woman's making the initial move:

**It shows outgoingness on her part. It also indicates that she is confident and assertive, all qualities I love in a woman.**

**I enjoy a woman who knows what she wants and has enough courage to say it.**

**I'm shy and an assertive woman makes things easier for me.**

**I like to know she is interested in me, because it takes a lot of pressure off me.**

**It lets me know she's liberated.**

**I'm generally a shy person and not too good at seducing women, so every little bit of help she's willing to offer is appreciated.**

**It indicates a potential for frank communication that can lead to a very adventurous, exciting liaison.**

By reaching out, you will give yourself and the man you meet a chance to start your relationship off on the right track.

*Give Him a Chance to Spoil and Want You*

Once you are sure a man wants you, sit back and enjoy the result of your work. Let him spoil you. **"My greatest pleasure in life is to please my woman, in and out of bed,"** says an executive in Boston. (He is only one of hundreds of respondents who told us this.)

One question asked in the survey was: After a night of passion, do you like to:

| | |
|---|---|
| Make breakfast with her | 62% |
| Prepare breakfast for her | 33% |
| Be served breakfast in bed | 5% |

For a man it's extremely important to please and impress a woman, anytime, anywhere. Therefore:

- Don't offer to pay for half of the romantic dinner you just enjoyed. That you earn as much as he is no reason he can't be generous. If the relationship becomes more lasting, or if you marry, you will certainly get your chance to pay your share.
- Don't worry about whether:
  - he can afford the present he just gave you
  - he is taking too much time off work for you
  - he has time to see you this week (if he doesn't, he'll tell you)

Instead, enjoy his admiration and give him time to desire you.

And when your mutual desire leads you to the bedroom, don't make it a habit. Let him be uncertain whether you will make love when you get together. A salesman from Kansas explains why this is preferable:

> My girlfriend, Donna, a pretty brunette, insisted that we make love every time we saw each other. When the pressure of her demands made me nearly impotent, I decided to ask

**her why she thought we had to make
love each time. She was very surprised by my question and said,
"Oh, I thought you wanted it."**

(Fortunately for Donna, this relationship was
saved because her man spoke up. Otherwise
she might have lost him.)

Nobody likes to feel obliged to have sex or
to know that it's too easily available. The
things that are harder to get are more appreciated, and help keep the mystery alive.

*Be Sure That What You Get Is What You Want*

Disappointments, insecurities, and doubts
often make us settle for less than we deserve.
When you find a man you're attracted to,
don't let your feelings run away with you.
Try to keep cool and stand back a little. Learn
as much as possible about him. Never—even
if he turns out to be perfect in every way—
think for one moment how *lucky* you are to
have him. He is equally *lucky* to have you.

One way to stay out of an unhappy relationship, one that doesn't fit your needs, is to
look at your life and make sure that you are
not doing something only as a means to dis-
tract you from a problem. Look at where you
are and why you are there. For example,
Lisa, a young woman with a small child, had
just gone through a divorce. She got seriously involved with a man she met at a ball

game. She was so grateful that somebody wanted her that she didn't consider if he was what she really needed. The affair didn't last very long, and when it was over, she felt worse than before. Her already acute feeling of being a failure deepened, and her chances for a happy relationship diminished.

Many women seem to be victims of bad luck where men are concerned. But is it really misfortune? A little luck never hurts, but that's not the determining factor in the following case. Marilyn, a good-looking, voluptuous redhead, was married to four men, all of whom gave her a hard time and made her life miserable. After her last divorce she teamed up with a man who is no different from the four who preceded him. A woman like this obviously doesn't think that she has any control over whom she spends her time with, and stays with men with whom she is unhappy.

Having the right mate is such an important part of our lives that we should pay a lot more attention to the initial stages of a relationship. This is when the tone is set for what happens later. Ironically, this is the period when we are the most lenient, ready to accept things that make us miserable later. Failure cannot always be prevented, but at least give yourself a chance to avoid it. Let your mind speak as much as your feelings.

*Don't Think of Men as All Alike*

Preconceived ideas and affairs gone sour make us categorize men. We make generalizations about the entire male population. Resentment leads us to say things like: "Men are all the same, they have only one thing in mind," or "Men are less sensitive than women."

The truth is, we use these generalizations as a defense, but they don't serve us well because they prevent us from finding the exceptions. Listen to the men themselves: **"Not all men are the same—give us a chance." "Never assume anything about a guy, ask!"** No one, either male or female, likes to be regarded as the same as everyone else. All our lives we try to establish our identities. **"We are all individuals and should be regarded as such."**

Susan and Dick worked for the same company. She had had a crush on him for years, but he was a married man. When she heard of his divorce, she told him how sorry she was. A few weeks later they started to go out together. Their relationship lasted more than a year. During this time Dick had asked her several times to marry him, but based on her previous experience with a divorced man, she refused, thinking that he needed more time to make such an important decision. Can you imagine her surprise when one day he told her that they were through because he was going to get married?

When you meet a man, don't draw parallels. Don't think, "Oh, he's just like George," because he isn't, he's Dick. He's another human being with characteristics all his own, and he deserves to be given a chance—which only *you* can give him.

## Determine What Sex Really Means to You

Sex has as many different meanings as love, and often we don't realize what it means to us. Not because we can't figure it out, but simply because we have never asked ourselves. We tend to accept sex to be what we have heard and learned about it—a necessity of some sort—without ever questioning if it applies to us.

For some of us sex can be a pick-me-up, for others it is a confirmation of our attractiveness, and yet others take it for love.

One woman who had casual sex about once a week felt disappointed and let down afterward. To avoid this kind of pitfall, you need to take a good look at what sex means to you. Ask yourself these questions:

- Are sex and love one in my mind?
- Can I have sex with a man without loving him?
- Does sex also mean cuddling and hugging, just being close to a man?
- Can I live without, or with very little, sex?

- What sacrifices would I be willing to make for good sex?
- To what extreme would I go to find any sex?

Don't think you are above these questions because your intellect tells you that you can do without sex. Admitting that you do need it once a month (or more often) will give you a different perspective on how to handle your sex life and the men you need and want for it.

And if you're married, being honest about your needs will certainly improve your marriage. **"Being more open about your desires and intentions can only improve a relationship"** is the opinion of a mailman in Florida.

Knowing the answers to questions like the ones above will make you aware that your actions are a result of *your* desires and *your* choices. This is an instrumental step in gaining self-confidence.

**Don't be afraid to be a woman. Get in touch with your emotions, your wants, and dislikes, and follow through with them. Going to bed with a man simply because you want him to like you, not because you really want to be there and share in the experience, will be damaging to the relationship in the long run.**

29

*Be More Knowledgeable About Sex*

This message was communicated by many men without claiming to be great experts themselves. **"In sexual matters and matters of the heart, everyone, including myself, could stand to be more aware,"** writes a thirty-two-year-old electrician from Illinois. They did feel, though, that their interest in sex made them more open and knowledgeable. Furthermore, they have not suggested that women can learn about sex only by changing partners. What they did recommend, besides having an open mind, was that women "read more men's magazines, especially the letters from readers, and maybe some books about lovemaking. This will help them understand more fully the wide scope of sex."

Donald had been reading *Penthouse* since his college days. He continued to do so when he got married, but he didn't dare to bring the magazine home, knowing how strict Marlene, his wife, had been brought up. He read them in the office, or while on a trip in his hotel room.

Marlene loved her husband and was a good wife, but when it came to sex she always felt inadequate. Her prudish background left her ill-prepared for that part of her life. She wondered how Donald knew so much, but she didn't dare to ask, fearing that her ignorance might show.

One day she was unpacking her husband's

suitcase and found a copy of *Penthouse*. She was shocked. How could he read magazines like this? Indignant, she decided to confront him. However, she couldn't resist opening it, and looking at the pictures, she thought them to be in bad taste. Then she started to read; to her surprise there were letters and articles which answered some of her questions. They also made her realize that others had some of the same problems.

By the time Donald came home, she had changed her mind about confronting him. She instead put the magazine casually on a table. When he saw it, he looked at her anxiously, remembering that he had forgotten to take it out of his suitcase. Not wanting to admit how useful she had found the information in *Penthouse*, she said, "Darling, you don't have to read this when you are away from home, you can read it right here. You know I'm a grown-up girl." Donald took her in his arms and hugged her, thankful for her understanding.

But his gratitude is not her only reward for overcoming her hang-ups. Reading the magazine from time to time gives her a different viewpoint about sex. It makes her share and enjoy their lovemaking as an equal partner.

It is indeed surprising that our Western civilization, which prides itself on its sophistication and worldliness, allows us to start our adult lives without giving us instructions about sex, one of the most important human functions. In Eastern cultures women are trained in the art of making love, and an art it is, which some women such as the famous courtesans have made into a lifestyle.

But coming back to the men's suggestions that women be more familiar with the subject of sex, let me emphasize again that it does not stem from selfishness, but rather from wanting women to enjoy sex as much as they do.

If we are badly prepared, the only thing to do is learn. You may not find it easy to read *Penthouse* or *Playboy* at first, but once you get over the first shock it will become easier and more fun (and you don't have to read every issue). Knowing what the competition is up to never hurts. Besides, these glossy, naked girls are no threat to you—they aren't with your man, *you* are!

*Don't Ever Think of Sex as Dirty or Bad*

This is the advice many respondents gave. It often sounded more like a plea, and, sad to report, according to the remarks men hear during foreplay or lovemaking, there are indeed women who think it is.

- "I feel so dirty now."
- "Don't get that stuff all over me."
- "Look at the mess you made."
- "Don't get messy."

Any woman who feels that the sperm of her partner is dirty must not be in love with him. Of course, sex can be distasteful or even dirty, but in a caring relationship between a man and woman, it should never be seen as unclean. Thinking it is will do irrevocable damage to a man's feelings as well as inhibiting the woman from reaching full sexual satisfaction.

The question to ask here is: How can any woman who regards sex as dirty make love to a man without losing her self-respect?

**"Sex is not bad in itself, and when rightly used is the key to an enriched life and a pattern of enjoyment,"** a Connecticut physician feels.

## CHAPTER TWO

# Combining Sex and Love

"Love in bed can only get so good, but love out of bed can always get better." This was the comment of a real estate broker in California. An insurance salesman from Massachusetts sees it this way:

> People forget that good sex is a by-product of a good loving relationship. One of the reasons there are so many screwed-up (no pun intended) people in the world is that they think that if they make love like rabbits, they have a good relationship. Much to their chagrin, they find that this isn't so.

And still other men say:

> A woman should be familiar with sex and be able to satisfy both her man and herself. The other quality you must have is knowing how to live—to have fun when the

time is right, whether it's going to dinner, taking a trip, or just running in the park. But when the time comes to be serious, have some concern and constructive input, whatever the situation may be.

Remember to put sex in its proper place. It's only part of a relationship and of life. Enjoy it but don't overemphasize it.

One-night stands can be a great release for sexual tension, but I believe that a woman who shows her feelings to her man and vice versa is a great sexual turn-on for both. And knowing that someone loves you is the greatest turn-on of them all.

Whichever way we look at it, sex alone is not the answer, but neither is only love. The secret of a *lasting* relationship lies in how well we can combine and balance the two. Merging these two basic human needs successfully is the biggest challenge in our lives. With enough love and a healthy sex drive it can be done.

*Aim to Please*

"Seeing that I please a woman, sexually and otherwise, is the biggest turn-on of all." This attitude was expressed many times. Do you know why this situation is such a turn-on?

Being liked by others is important to most

of us, male or female. It confirms that what we do and stand for is accepted, even admired. Listen closely and you may be surprised at how often people say things like: "I think he likes me" or "I guess she cares" in referring only to daily encounters—not their personal lives, where this assurance is even more essential.

In relationships with men, knowing that we please is like getting high. It boosts our ego and puts us on cloud nine.

Can we influence how much we are liked? We certainly can. It takes some effort and thoughtfulness, as well as sincerity. Here is the advice of a twenty-six-year-old married navel officer stationed in South Carolina: **"Always give a little more than you get, and in the end you get back just as much and probably more."**

Start testing this method in your everyday life. Whenever you think someone doesn't like you, make an extra effort to be pleasant. Most of the time you'll be surprised by the reaction you get. Maybe the other person thought that you didn't like him or her.

During a bridge tournament Jane was playing against a man who was not friendly or even polite. It made the game more difficult and took some of the fun out of it. However, since she had no idea why he behaved so discourteously, she decided that she wouldn't allow him to spoil her fun. She was pleasant and ignored his behavior.

During the cocktail hour which followed the match he came to her and apologized for his rudeness, and went on to explain that some business problems were the reason for his impolite manners. If Jane had just assumed that the man did not like her and had reacted to him instead of ignoring his rudeness, she would have spoiled her day and never found out that he liked her after all.

When it comes to the man in your life, use the same method. Never jump to conclusions as to why he might be unfriendly or distant. Don't think: "What's the matter with him now?" Be kind and sincere, and try to find out why he's reacting as he is. He'll be grateful for your understanding and will repay you through love.

*Keep Romance Alive*

**"Men are as romantic as women, but we can't show it as easily—which might be the reason why we rely on women to show us the way."**

Romance is the all-important link between love and sex. If you let it slip away, your efforts to combine the two will come to little or nothing. As we will see in the following chapters, men are as much affected by romance as women are. They show themselves susceptible to the sound of the waves, the stars, fireplaces, even the backseats of Chevys. But romance goes much deeper than this; it's a way of looking at life.

Romance has the magic to make us dream. It helps us believe in our plans and makes illusion look like reality. It lets us express what we otherwise would have difficulties finding the words for. Returning with your man to the place your first met is a romantic way of telling him how glad you are that you did. Standing with him outside for a few minutes to look at the stars on a particularly clear night provides a moment of closeness. Planning a short trip for just the two of you (even if you never go) shows how much you want to be alone with him. Looking after him whenever he leaves you and waving to him says: "I miss you already." And don't forget to give him a compliment now and then; it means that you still find him as wonderful as when you met.

Being romantic also means keeping negative thoughts out of your mind during intimate moments. They serve no purpose other than to worry you, and won't improve any situation. Stay positive and see the good side of things. Don't let the glow fade.

If you catch yourself thinking that romance is appropriate only for young lovers, put the thought out of your head, because it belongs to anyone who loves someone.

*Don't Become One of the Boys*

To be feminine is not degrading—for women are the only ones to do it properly. Take pride in yourself and your man will have the staying power, not only in love-making, but also in fidelity, his occupation, and his family life.

At a time when women are finally gaining some equality in the workplace, please remind yourselves that you needn't become one of the guys to do it. I've seen probably hundreds of women compromising their femininity in the workplace, particularly in roles that until a few years ago were traditionally male. Business suits and the like are fine and dandy. No one expects you to look like Scarlett O'Hara for a day at the office, but why not wear a soft blouse with that suit? Sure, let them know you're more than just a pretty face, but don't go to the other extreme by becoming just another "smart girl." If the only compliments you've received lately are on your work, maybe you need to take a look at yourself and reevaluate.

Remember that, even though it's the 20th century and women can get more respect for what they are, a man is still a man and a woman is still a woman.

**Quit trying to be equal at all times. Enjoy being a woman, and let your man spend money and time on you.**

These comments confirm that women should not shed their femininity in order to lead a professional life. What men ask is that a woman stays aware of her womanly resources. **"Being intelligent and independent is wonderful; so is being a woman!"**

*Never Take Your Partner for Granted*

The routine of everyday life can make us lose sight of what is really important. When we're busy or tired, we forget about the little niceties. Sometimes we even skip being polite to those we love.

Perhaps it's a false security that misleads us. It's a dangerous trap for married people or those involved in serious relationships to assume that your mate will still put up with you no matter what. Don't relax too much. Love as well as sex needs nurturing and attention.

If you feel that your relationship or sex life has eroded, talk to your man and ask for his reaction.

**Never take a man for granted. Find out what would please him, and start doing it.**

**Being taken for granted makes you wonder if she still cares.**

**It makes you feel like a part of the household furniture.**

To avoid giving him this impression, be more attentive. Don't forget simple thanks. If he remembered to buy milk, or got home early, or replaced a light bulb without being asked, let him know you appreciate it.

And when you ask him to do something, don't make it sound like a command. After all, he isn't obliged to do anything. "I'd appreciate it if you'd call the insurance company today—I'm really worried about our claim" sounds a lot better than "Are you ever going to call Metropolitan?"

Appreciation, acknowledging what your partner does, is an important ingredient in combining love and sex. It is also one that doesn't require much effort—just a little thoughtfulness.

*Be Loving after Sex*

A solid loving relationship needs hugging, touching, stroking, and kissing as much as it needs sex. A good time to show your affection is after the waves of passion have subsided. **"The way a woman responds to a man after making love tells him more than any words. And when a woman respects herself and her body, then she should never have any problems in showing her partner her love."**

41

The sexual act is our most intimate communication, and we should show our feelings for our partner as much after it as before. Before an orgasm, all of us are enthusiastic, but showing tenderness and affection afterward says a lot about how much you love your partner. First, it says, "I love you as much now as earlier," erasing any doubts that the attraction might have been only a sexual one. Second, it tells the other person that what he just did was very good. **"Gently hugging and kissing is a way of saying thank you."**

Remarks like **"Would you turn on the television?"** or **"Pass me my cigarettes"** do not reassure your partner that what just happened was significant. One respondent wrote sadly: **"After lovemaking she doesn't say a word. I have to ask or she just turns around and goes to sleep. I would rather have a question or a hug and a kiss."**

Here's a good piece of advice: **"After the climax, a woman should not get up right away, but keep the man inside her until he is ready to exit. Then she should gently stroke the man and talk softly to him."**

Most men feel closer to a woman after sex and find her even more desirable. **"Be warm and loving"** is a frequent request for afterplay, which can easily become foreplay again. Even when it doesn't, holding him in your arms and stroking his face or his body will allow the mood of the moment to linger.

*Love Your Partner for What He Is*

Often couples find that their partner does not seem as "perfect" as when they first met. When we know someone well we start to see past the surface and conclude that "he is not the man I married," or thoughts to that effect. But he is! Your initial infatuation is simply giving way to a more realistic picture. Brian has always spent too much time in the bathroom, gone bowling on Thursdays, and been a bit of a hypochondriac. He has not become another person, you're just seeing him differently.

Once you've overcome the shock of discovering the facts, you have to think positively and remember the qualities that attracted you to him in the first place. Most likely they are still there, but you have lost sight of them by concentrating on your new discoveries.

Here's a viewpoint from a boutique owner in New York: **"Don't do what many men do. There is too much image-seeking on both sides, trying to find the Mr. Macho or beauty queen. People are people and should be loved for themselves."**

**"If you don't have a Tom Selleck or a Robert Wagner, don't overlook the real advantages of the average man. Most regular-looking men will become beautiful when you get to know them,"** says a professor of computer science.

Loving someone with all his faults and

showing him that you do is truly a way of combining love and sex. Anyone can love perfection, but it's in short supply. And looking at things from his point of view, he has to put up with your imperfections, too.

*Participants' Suggestions How to Be a Better Lover*

Question 38 of the survey was: If you had to give one suggestion to women regarding how to be better lovers, what would it be?

If I had to give one suggestion, it would be the age-old advice of mothers to their daughters: "Massage their egos a little." After all, I, and many other men, make it a point to compliment women we are with. The least they could do is reciprocate.

Put simply, men are creatures like yourselves: some frail, some strong. We all have similar feelings, thoughts, and desires, and if we look at each other with some openness so that we can see into each other without so much complexity, we can all find love.

Communicate! A man never feels more a man than when he's with a woman, pleasing her, fulfilling mutual needs and desires.

Be more confident in yourself. Accept your feelings and listen to them. Sex is the most natural thing since birth.

Let a man know when he is doing something you like (in and out of the bedroom). Reassure him, lead him with subtle hints. At the same time let him explore and experiment so that his discoveries (which you lead him to) appear to be natural. It is through satisfying her that I'm truly satisfied.

I address my advice to both men and women: Observe the golden rule. We all want pretty much the same thing: dignity, self-esteem, sexual gratification. We all want our individuality appreciated, we all want to feel lovable and loved. Sex is beautiful and right. Give and you will receive. It is a blessed capacity for pleasure that is ours to use caringly. Forget the lovers you've had before, forget techniques. Operate on feedback from the one you're with. Appreciate each person as an individual just like yourself. Learn to care. There is no such thing as a universal "great lover." There are only people who, aware of their own needs and those of others, create and surrender to the best there is in sex.

Stop immediately regarding sex as something a woman gives to a man (for whatever reason). Try to see it for what it is—a pleasurable activity two people engage in for mutual satisfaction, with warmth, respect, and regard for each other.

I hope that more people will learn to know themselves for what they are: a special person with inner qualities which allow us to devote ourselves mentally and sexually to a satisfying and rewarding love. This can carry two people, like a swift velvet cloud, through all the hard times, setbacks, and troubles, which may seem unbearable until we give one another without inhibitions what is important.

Find someone you can relax and enjoy lovemaking with. Find out what turns both of you on and then do it. Don't be afraid of variety or openness. Good lovemaking is the best part of being human. Never burden your bed with other people's expectations or opinions (except your partners). The only true perversions are guilt and hurting your partner. (I intend to give this advice to my son as well as my daughter.)

The majority of women could be more up-front about who they are on a personal level, more honest with themselves and less macho. Too many women playact in bed.

Don't be shy, do things to your partner that will turn him on and get him excited. Also, if a woman feels good about the way she looks and what she is doing, then she will enjoy her sexual experience more, and so will her partner.

To be a better lover, learn how to go down on a man. So few women know how. The important ingredient here is desire. It's so easy and enjoyable to teach a lover to do this if she enjoys it too. In addition, she should show or tell me what brings her to climax—that's a real high for me.

Learn to give good head; that is, in the sense that oral intercourse is a giving experience. What makes sex good is due as much to the pleasure you give as the pleasure you get, and giving head means deriving pleasure from the pleasure you cause. The more the woman actually enjoys the touch and feeling of a penis, the better it will be. The women I've know who did this were good because they were inventive and creative. They knew the pleasure they were giving, and it made them feel good.

Take my seven-day course—no, just kidding. I think a woman should be more honest in bed without coming across as demanding or pushy. This way she can allow her lover to satisfy her as completely as possible, which for myself and a majority of other men I know is a major turn-on.

A man's prowess is satisfied when his partner has a real orgasm, or is at least writhing in ecstasy from something he has done. My personal experience has shown that a woman is at her best as a lover when she gets what she wants. Then the reciprocal feelings come back to her man most naturally. Honesty in bed definitely makes a better lover!

My advice is—relax and enjoy! It's a whole lot easier to be happy than sad.

## CHAPTER THREE

# Keeping a Man by Loving Him

Finding a man is easier than keeping one. In the beginning of a relationship or a marriage, Cupid carries us over the initial bumps. He blinds us with romance and desire, and even makes us believe that we will live happily ever after. But to make it come true we have to do more than just believe in love. We have to work for it every day, all year around.

**Loving is like dancing. You need a good partner and you need a good leader. The leader in the department of emotions is without doubt the woman. It seems as if nature has equipped her better to handle emotions and to support her man.**

It is indeed a tall order to take the lead in emotional matters, but the role is one that should make every woman feel proud of herself and increase her self-esteem and confidence. It is regrettable, therefore, that not all women are aware of this gift and the importance that comes with it.

Learning to recognize and respect each other's strengths makes relationship between men and women less confusing. A step in the right direction, leading to better understanding, is to acknowledge your own strength and to start by using it with the one you love.

### Make a Commitment, Help Your Man to Love You

**"Loving someone takes a dedicated commitment, compromise, and a determination to succeed. It is truly a partnership. Two people can make it work, but it only takes one to really screw it up!"** This sad but true statement comes from a doctor in Michigan. When starting an affair or a more binding relationship with a man you like, you have to make a commitment to yourself to make it work.

It's not unusual today to hear a woman complain that the man she's dating is not ready to make a commitment. But how ready is she? Has she done her part? Has she shown him that she cares without giving him the impression of being desperate to catch him?

Commitment should never be confused with possessiveness. Pressing someone usually makes them feel that they have no choice and therefore they feel trapped. However, if you wish to be truly committed to a relationship, you must be understanding and prepared to accept what it takes to make the relationship work. "If you don't press him, and give him time, your commitment will eventually get him."

**"Help your man in his quest to love you. Don't make him struggle in your relationship"** is what a twenty-nine-year-old computer programmer wrote us. A married technician from Utah, thirty-nine, sees it this way: **"Women need to understand more about men. A man is a human being who needs the same things that women need: affection, respect, and most of all to be loved. Don't always expect him to be the lover."**

An insurance claim adjuster from New Hampshire offered this advice: **"Act as if the man you're with is the one and only, that you need and want him more than anything or anyone. Then your love will be repaid many times and in many ways."**

**"Show at least a little love—men need to be loved"** was the cry of another.

What these men are referring to is not sex, but affection and understanding. They need to know that someone is in their corner rooting for them, supporting them, and loving them for what they are. **"If you want to receive, you must give. Share your thoughts and feelings, show that you're committed, and you'll have little trouble being loved."**

*Be His Friend and Trust Him*

"**Be your lover's best friend—it's very important in making a relationship work.**" Similar advice came from another respondent: "**Everyone, including us men, needs someone to unburden themselves to, releasing stress and pressure. Who could be better than the woman you love and feel comfortable with?**"

This is what men would like, but their replies indicate that not many women are ready to assume this role. Some women are even wary of men who need to unburden themselves, seeing it as a weakness.

Why are women more sympathetic to other women and their problems than to their man? Has the stereotyped macho image really convinced women that men can handle the problems of life alone, or that they should? The results of the survey clearly show that besides a lover a man needs a friend. Finding this in one and the same person is what every man is looking for. "**Friendship, companionship, and someone to listen to us is what men want most from a relationship, besides sex.**" (Note that sex is not in first place here.) "**Be his friend when he needs you. When he is angry, let him blow off steam. Don't get back at him, support him.**"

When it comes to trust, the majority of respondents agree with a remark Dr. Joyce Brothers once made: "The best proof of love is trust." This is true for emotional as well as for physical love.

Who else do you know as intimately as your man? He has seen you in all kind of situations; happy, sad, and passionate. He knows you as well as you know him. If you don't trust him, he will never be able to support you to your satisfaction. And don't forget the harm it can do. This young man from Tampa asked:

> **Doesn't she trust me enough to tell me when she doesn't feel like making love and explain to me why? Do I look so insensitive?**
> Another said:
> **I can accept that my wife doesn't always feel like sex because it happens to me too. What I can't accept is that she thinks she has to lie, that she doesn't think I'm worth the truth.**

Trust can even be a turn-on, a proof of love that will make life a lot easier on an everyday basis. A salesman from South Texas, thirty-five years old, has this to say: "**A great turn-on is trust. For instance, being asked to pick up a box of tampons. After all, she's sharing with me the most personal and feminine part of her life by asking and trusting my discretion and help with her personal needs.**"

Trust really translates into being so comfortable with a man that you don't need to pretend. You can be yourself, you know he will understand, you know he is your friend. Dealing with him in this way, asking him to do things for you, including him in all aspects of your life is a compliment for him. Therefore, never *assume* he won't do something for you. Ask him. Show him that your trust him.

Another way to be trusting is not to be unduly jealous. A radio announcer from Florida tells us why:

> **Don't be mad at your man for looking at other women. It proves he's human. What matters is whom he is with. Faithfulness is not sticking to your side every minute and only having eyes for you, but noticing all the other women and returning to you.**

### Don't Mother Him

The unconditional love of a mother, even for the adult male, is something he looks for and needs. But as an adult he wants it without the advice or parental domination. **"I don't want a woman to be a mother to me, even if I want her to be ready to talk some sense into me every now and then,"** comments a thirty-six-year-old security officer in Tampa. In other words, we must be ready with advice, but give it only when asked.

I once had a male friend who gave me the

following answer whenever I offered advice:
"When I need help, you'll be the first to
know." I felt hurt. Once or twice I reacted
angrily, which didn't get me anywhere and
made matters worse. Trying to avoid these
remarks, and, more important, trying to keep
myself from getting hurt, I took another look
at what I was doing. I had to admit that
in fact I had been telling him what to do
without having been asked for my opinion.
I was trying to justify myself with the time-
honored excuse, "I only meant well," when
I remembered the phrase: "The most harm
in the world is done by people who mean
well."

Verbal help is not the only maternal assist-
ance that is better withheld. In the interest of
good relationships, here are a few don'ts:

- "I don't want my clothes laid out every day."
- "I don't want my bags packed when I
  go on a trip."
- "I hate when a woman flicks hair or
  lint off my jacket when we are in
  public."
- "I get along fine when my wife is
  away. There is no need to worry and
  fuss."
- "I don't want her to serve me my drink
  all the time. I enjoy serving her now
  and then."

Feeling independent is as important for men as it is for women. Also, remember that a healthy balance in a relationship can not be retained if one of you assumes a role of authority.

*Show Your Love Through Little Things*
**"Spoil your husband/boyfriend with surprises such as little notes, presents, or a call while he is at work. Prepare good dinners, because finally the way to a man's heart is through his stomach."** This is the advice of a government employee from Washington, D.C.

Why are little things so important? Simply because there aren't that many big ways in which we can show how much we love somebody. But everyday life offers endless opportunties to express our feelings, to let him see that we have thought of him while he was away, that we have missed him, that we love him. Our signs of affection and love can vary from cooking a man's favorite meal to getting tickets for a baseball game or wearing a dress he likes.

A young man from Tulsa wrote: **"I'm a bicycle racer and having my legs massaged every day is something I really appreciate."** A manager of a manufacturing firm in Chicago gives this hint: **"Phone your man during the day and tell him what you are going to do to him that night—then do it!"**

If you can't think of anything your man

would like: "Put yourself in his place, treat him as you would like to be treated. Think what would please you, and try it out on him. You'll be surprised how these so-called 'little things' can bring romance back into your life."

A man from Pennsylvania summarizes it like this: **"Show your love for your man in your own special way. It was the reason why he was attracted to you in the first place, and that is why he will continue to love you."**

When Betty and Phil were engaged, they both worked in the city. She finished work half an hour before him and used this time to walk to his office to pick him up. After a day of work Phil couldn't think of anything else he wanted more than to see Betty waiting for him.

Today she doesn't work anymore, and they don't live in the city, but from time to time Betty makes the effort to come to town to meet her man. Not only does it recall moments of their youth and love, but it says that she still cares as much.

We should all try to remember from time to time what it was that attracted him to us. Are we still dressing to please him? Are we still sending funny little cards? Are we still writing messages with our lipstick on the bathroom mirror? If you write no more than yes on your list, it might be time to revive the past.

*Be Gentle and Patient*

In or out of bed, being gentle and patient will gain you something that all women yearn for—tenderness! When a man is treated with patience and compassion he will relax, and won't be afraid of showing you his vulnerable side.

Squeezing his hand or stroking his hair at the right moment can sometimes bring you closer to him than making love.

**I like a woman who will hold me while we are watching television or when we have gone to bed. I don't have to make love to her every time we touch. Just being held while we are falling asleep makes me feel more loved then if we had spent the same time making love.**

**Just a simple kiss when it is not expected tells me that she still finds me attractive.**

A twenty-six-year-old personnel officer from Dallas asks this question:

**How many women realize just how much it means to a man to receive a kiss—on the neck, cheek, forehead, anywhere—that's unsolicited, on the spur of the moment? Just a little kiss, sincere and impassioned, hardly more than a peck, or even a short, tight hug**

**can stir a man's heart more than hours of lovemaking.**

But when the hugging has progressed to making love, patience is as necessary as before, if not more so. A pilot from Vancouver wrote, **"Nothing works under pressure. If a man feels he had better get a hard-on fast or his partner is going to be disappointed, she will be nine times out of ten."**

A Brooklyn accountant gave this advice to the woman making love to a man for the first time: **"Don't expect too much from him. Don't laugh or belittle him if he is overexcited and impotent. Try to be patient, it can only get better."** And two other appeals:

**Go slow, we aren't as horny all the time as some women think.**

**Put yourself in the place of your lover— you don't always feel like it either.**

*Share Your Joys and Sorrows with Him— Communicate*

If you want to spend your life with a man, you have to be able to share things, and the only way to do this is through communication. In fact, the advice of one respondent was a single word written in big letters several times on a page: **"Communicate, Communicate, Communicate!"** It reflected what hundreds of others said. Communicating includes sharing simple, small things and events with each other. Never think that this or that is unimportant. As long as it is part of your life together, share it. It is impossible to truly know someone if you don't have open communication.

Lack of it will not only make your life lonely, but can result in loss of love, or the breakup of a marriage. By the time you're at that point, it is usually too late to see that a little more sharing, a little more talk, a little more openness could have avoided the heartache.

**"Collect and share—a union is a work of art that is never quite finished"** are the words of a hairdresser in New Orleans. Lucky are the couples who have that type of a relationship. If you don't, make the effort; try to reach out to your man before it's too late. You might not get a response right away, but keep trying, because as a store owner from Toronto explains: **"Men are really not as insensitive as we are made out to be, just a little hard of hearing at times."**

How should you start? Ask him how his day was. You may get just a "fine" or an "OK." Be insistent: "Who did you see today? What did you do? Is everything all right at work?" He might be a little surprised at your sudden interest, but ignore it. When he has answered your questions, tell him a little about what you did.

Opening the lines of communication is like prying open a door, and it should be done a little at a time. Don't get discouraged, just keep pushing—gently. Once the lines of communication have been opened, it's easier to share the little pleasures and worries as well as the big ones, pulling you closer and closer together.

One other piece of advice came from a forty-six-year-old executive in Kansas:

> **When your man does something that upsets you, don't walk away hurt. Say right away that you don't appreciate what he did or said. Not speaking up will make a big thing out of something that could have been taken care of right away. Keeping things bottled up will make you angry and resentful, and when eventually you speak up, I might not even remember what you are angry about.**

### Don't Criticize a Man in Bed—Be Aware of His Fragile Ego

"Understand the male ego—it's all he has," confesses an executive in New York, who speaks for the majority. Another said: "A man functions on his ego—build it."

Women are not responsible for weak male egos, but we have to live with them, and being aware of how men react and why will help us to understand them better. The old cliché "Flattery will get you anywhere" owes its success to fragile egos, which need stroking and boosting. Any woman who has perfected the art of complimenting a man will always get what she wants.

Unfortunately, this survey showed that men don't get as many compliments as they would like. On the contrary, when reading what some women say to their men while making love, one can only hope that it is said out of thoughtlessness, because one doesn't need a fragile ego to be hurt by remarks like these:

- "You're too short, you can't keep an erection, you don't please me."
- "Your penis is too small."
- "Please hurry up, I'm tired."
- "Well, what are you waiting for?"
- "Hurry up and get it over with."
- "How am I going to explain this? Look at the mess you made."
- "Is sex all you want from me? Are you ever going to come?"
- "Are you all through yet?"
- "Don't touch me there, it's dirty!"
- "Oh, God, I feel guilty about going to bed with you."
- "Uh, this is the part I hate the most."
- "Stop, I'm not that kind of girl."
- "What are you going to do with that little thing?"

- "It sure took a long time, you're sweaty, get off me."
- "I wish you had a bigger penis."

No, a woman shouldn't go along with anything a man wants, but find other ways to say no, ways that are less hurtful, less critical. Remember the advice given earlier: **"Put yourself in your partner's place."** If the women quoted above had followed this precept, they would have done less damage.

And don't think that a man will forget this kind of criticism once out of the bedroom—not at all. He will probably try to protect himself against other attacks by being more closed and distant than before. If you have complaints or would like him to do something differently, tell him outside the bedroom (see Chapter 6).

CHAPTER FOUR

# Keeping a Man Through
# the Power of Sex

The sexual power nature has bestowed upon women is a precious gift. It allows a woman to be in control of her relationships, and allows her to make the man she loves and herself happy. It gives her the privilege to choose her partner—and to have him do what she wants.

History has proven many times that the power of sex is strong enough to make empires tumble, to alter the course of lives and nations drastically—just think of Anthony and Cleopatra!

Unfortunately, not all women are aware of, or know how to use, this special gift; as witness, this question from a forty-nine-year-old president of a Fortune 500 company in Los Angeles: **"Why aren't women aware of the power they have over men?"**

If you doubt that we have that power, just

think of the men you know who worship their wives or lovers. Have you ever asked yourself why he adores her? Or did you think that she was just lucky to find such a loving man? In most cases luck doesn't have much to do with it. What you are looking at is a sexually satisfied man whose woman knows how to please him. She uses her sexual powers to bewitch him.

Another respondent had this comment: **"It's hard to believe that women don't make more use of the influence they have on men; used rightly they could get anything they want from us."**

Courtesans were always aware of their influence and made good use of it. It got them what they wanted, even kings. Not that there are many kings around today, but the man we love should certainly be the most important person in our lives. And look what treating him as such will get us: **"After a night of passion in which my woman has loved me to the best of her ability, I treat her like a princess."** That is the promise of a forty-two-year-old doctor from Atlanta.

Woody Allen, in his film *A Midsummer Night's Sex Comedy*, put it this way: "When a man's sperm count is low, he doesn't listen to reason, but when the sperm count is high, he'll do anything for you."

So the secret of using one's sexual powers lies in keeping the sperm count high—high enough to make your man love and adore you, to convince him through your love-making that he will never need anyone else but you. And the way to do this is to know and satisfy his sexual needs. This doesn't mean you'll do anything he wants, but you'll guide his desires with an open and adventurous mind to mutual satisfaction.

*Fan the Flame of Desire*

Softly whispering and murmuring nice things into his ear will not only encourage his lovemaking, but also increase his pleasure and his desire for you. **"A little encouragement and positive comments can turn a mediocre or bad lover into one that is willing to try and try hard on pleasing his woman."**

Of the many nice things one can say, what specifically do men find pleasing and exciting? The following suggestions might be helpful for anyone who doesn't know how to verbalize admiration for a lover. They are all answers to the survey question: What kind of remarks will make you feel more aroused?

- **I'd sure like you to carry me off to bed."**
- **"Oh, I just love your hairy chest, and you have a cute behind, too—let's undress."**
- **"Whatever you're doing, don't stop."**

- "I don't have a good day unless I talk to you."
- "I wanted you for so long, take me please."
- "You feel so good, please don't stop."
- "I love your body."
- "Please hold me close to you."
- "You're getting me hot."
- "I love every inch of you."
- "I want to feel you inside me."
- "I love it when you touch me like that."
- "You smell good!"
- "You're driving me crazy, I can't wait."
- "You really know how to make love to a woman."
- "I can't get enough of you."
- "Lets go to bed and hold each other."
- "Your hands feel so good on my skin."
- "I want to be hugged, you turn me on."
- "I love your body, you have a beautiful penis."

This should give you some ideas to start with. Once you've tried out a few of these and seen the effect, your imagination will do the rest.

You might have noticed that there is one sentence missing from this list. But since it was mentioned by more than 80% of the men, it deserves to stand on its own. A twenty-six-year-old journalist from Illinois said it beautifully: **"The most arousing words to me are simply—I love you."**

*Enjoy Foreplay*

The preparation, and anticipation is at least half the fun of anything we do, but when it comes to lovemaking, foreplay is more than just anticipation. As one man wrote: **"How can anyone be a good athlete without exercise?"** For that matter, since we are making an analogy to sports here, a warmup period.

Warming up starts with little things: a look, a teasing glance, a sexual remark, stroking his chest. For many people, however, the word "foreplay" means sex, whereas it only implies and leads to making love. And unless you allow yourself and your lover the time to get warmed up, lovemaking is not what it should be. Remember, it's how you get there that makes being there better!

> **Women always complain of men rushing through sex, but they can also slow it down if they want. Good oral sex is important, or really taking time to make love to a man's erection with her hands will make him enjoy it more and hurry less.**

Our orgasms—how good they are and how long they last—are the result of the excitement we are able to create beforehand. A great number of our respondents told us that they would welcome more foreplay, and some said they would be grateful for a little (obviously they get none). **"Learn the fun of foreplay"** is the advice of an executive from Oklahoma.

There are countless ways to play, to warmup, and every woman has to find out what pleases her and her man most. But don't get the impression that unusual or kinky things are expected—not at all. What excites an industrial laborer from Ohio? **"I'm aroused by the sight of a woman walking around in the nude or in a piece of lingerie. I love to sit back and talk with her while she combs her hair or applies a touch of makeup—I revel in the joy of having a woman with me."**

That's one way to begin. When it comes to the touching stage we hear this advice:

**Concentrate on a man's whole body during foreplay.**

**Stroking and caressing me all over is as pleasurable as touching my cock.**

A man also sees foreplay as a time to find out what his partner wants; it gives him a chance to explore her body and vice versa.

Once you know somebody well, foreplay will be more intimate. Familiarity with his body will allow you to indulge yourself, and it will increase your sexual power over him—a power he sees only as your love for him. For a woman who is not aroused as often as her man, foreplay can be the answer. Start by snuggling up to him, allowing him to hold you, and chasing away interfering thoughts such as what you're going to prepare for supper. Foreplay will soon put you in the mood as well.

Once again, by pleasing your man you're also pleasing yourself.

### Be Adventurous and Responsive

**"I would definitely like my partner to be more adventurous. I would like to try new things and new places, and I would like her to enjoy it, too."** In a nutshell, that's what almost half of the men responded to the question: Would you like your partner to be sexually more:

| | |
|---|---|
| Adventurous | 48% |
| Initiatory | 22% |
| Responsive | 15% |
| Assertive | 15% |

**Don't be afraid to try something new and different.**

**Deviate more from accepted norms.**

**Don't always do things in the same way.**

Don't hesitate to try something a little out of the ordinary.

Really get into the lovemaking. Contribute just as much or more than the male. Be responsive and initatory. Let him know when he is pleasing you or how he can please you. Don't be afraid to tell your partner, it can only make things better for both of us.

Be more adventurous, move a lot more and get into it because if you do, the male will keep it going a lot longer.

Be more adventurous without getting pushy or demanding. Take an active part by vocalizing your desires. Initiate sessions or practices, and remain open to discussions aimed at improving the love life.

Try not to react negatively to something a little out of the ordinary. Not being adventurous, not being ready to try out a new position or technique could rob you and your partner of mutual pleasures. It could rob you of the power over him these things give you.

For some of us this means expanding our ideas of what's normal in sex. Furthermore, we might have to abandon our old notions of what is sinful or perverted. To make this a bit easier, just remember that between two people who love each other, nothing they both agree on is forbidden or wrong. On the contrary, nothing will bring two people closer together than sharing sexual experiences.

While I was discussing this point with one of the men who took part in the survey, he looked at me in desperation and said: "Why do women always think we want them to hang upside-down from a chandelier? Why don't they find out what we want? Most of the time it is nothing outlandish." Well, let's find out what exactly they have in mind:

Be on top of the man more often.

I love to try new methods of lovemaking—different positions, like taking her from the back, or using lubricants.

Let's do it standing up in front of the mirror.

Allowing me to lick her body.

Spreading her legs and letting me look at her.

To masturbate herself in front of me.

Be ready for a 69.

Before a woman can be adventurous, she has to be responsive, and here are comments on that point:

> I went through some early years where the women didn't move—ever. I think it had to do with their reputation and upbringing, but then I found one who not only moved, but moved with me—wow!

> A lot of women I've been with have been set in old-fashioned, moralistic ways of doing it in a "hurry up and see you later" way, which I regretted because I like to spend as much time with a woman as I can, and have her respond to me.

> Responsiveness is the biggest turn-on. I like a woman to meet my thrusts, and to enjoy sex in unusual positions.

What "unusual" generally indicates is making a change, not always making love in the same way. In the words of a forty-seven-year-old, married shoe manufacturer:

> Before deciding that you won't do something, make sure you know exactly what your man wants from you. It could be something you will enjoy, too. Just listening to him could prevent your sex life from deteriorat-

**ing. At least he'll have the feeling that you gave him a chance to talk about it.**

And here is what happens when a woman makes the effort: **"My wife recently began to read up on some sexual experiments, and I think we may be turning the corner. She had been strictly a nighttime sex partner, but we've just begun daytime exploits—what bliss!"**

*Vary Your Pillow Talk*

Opinions about what is pornographic are divided. However, the answers to the survey indicated that for most men just calling things by their names, or putting into words what is going on while making love, is regarded as pornographic. Do men like it?

The survey question was: Does pornographic language:

| | |
|---|---|
| Excite you | 83% |
| Shock you | 10% |
| Makes no difference | 7% |

**"I find it very exciting when a woman uses pornographic language. It makes me feel that I have her so turned on that she's going to say these things in spite of what she feels is, or is not, proper."**

Even though the response was overwhelmingly favorable, it has to be noted that this applies only during lovemaking.

**A vulgar woman will turn me off in most circumstances, but a woman who is usually not vulgar and who in the heat of the moment gets vulgar tends to be attractive.**

**Pornographic language excites me very much, but only during intimate moments.**

**In bed it excites me. Out of bed I don't want to hear it from a woman.**

**In general, it neither shocks nor excites me. On occasions, though, it makes for interesting variety and excitement.**

**Dirty talk leads men to hope that a woman is sexually uninhibited and as interested in sex as we are.**

Even a sentence like "I love to fuck you" isn't salacious, because we're not doing anything offensive. Language normally seen as taboo can be forbidden fruit, which is always sweet to the taste.

A thirty-seven-year-old married insurance salesmen summarizes it like this: **"Hearing a woman say, 'Your cock feels so good in me,' ignoring conventions of what a lady can say or not, is very exciting. The more specific she** can be, the better I like it. It makes me feel that I really turn her on."

*Indulge His Fantasies*

Most fantasies are just that—fantasies. They will never happen in reality. But allowing them to happen in our minds brings new dimensions to lovemaking.

Instead of being upset by the things your man might fantasize about, let him talk about it. Let him tell you what would excite him most. Find out what he has always dreamed of doing. Not only will you become his confidant, but you will learn what makes him tick sexually, and thus how to satisfy him. Never forget, knowledge is the power needed to control any situation in life.

A Montreal photographer advised: **"Lovemaking is not just physical, so pay some attention to mind games like fantasies; to understand better what men want, inform yourself by reading books or men's magazines."** Speaking of magazines like *Penthouse* and *Playboy*, their success lies in the fantasies they provide. Few women share this desire. Many women don't even want publications like those in their house. You don't have to display the latest issue on your coffee table, but having it—even if it's under the towels in the linen closet—will make your man realize that you're interested in and open toward sex, and he won't have to feel like a naughty schoolboy reading it away from home.

The statistics of *Penthouse* show that most copies are sold in airports and hotels, which is confirmed by statements like this: **"I could never read *Penthouse* at home, so I read it either in the office or when I'm on a trip."**

Of course, there are fantasies other than those offered in magazines. Your man might not need inspiration, but have his own ideas. In the height of passion he might say, like one of our respondents, **"I would like to see you make love to another man."**(!) Whatever you do, if you are shocked, don't show it; just moan softly and let it pass. He said it in an abandoned moment, and it added to his excitement. Once off cloud nine, he would undoubtedly be jealous if he saw you making love with another man. If you reminded him of his wish at another time, he would certainly say that he didn't mean it.

**Don't be inhibited about fantasies and unusual acts. Whatever turns you both on is OK, and don't be afraid to ask for anything you're not getting.**

**Listen to his fantasies. Experiment more and don't feel dirty or cheap when trying new things which may be taboo. Share feelings and desires.**

77

Other men suggested that women watch adult movies with them. Maybe it's not your favorite type of entertainment, but saying no will only make them seem more interesting. If you agree, he'll probably rent only one or two before their attraction pales. Of course, there is always the possibility that you might enjoy them and learn something from them, and that's good too. Sometimes seeing what others do makes you more comfortable with your own sexuality.

Here is how a forty-one-year-old department store buyer sees it:

**The unknown is and has always been our worst enemy, because what we don't know we can't accept. Many people waste their life hiding because they are afraid that their real self will shock others. But learning about other people, and especially your man, will show you that there is no reason to hide.**

Fantasies can also mean simple things. **"Go out and buy a sexy outfit, and surprise your man one night when he is sitting around watching television. Walk in on him all dressed up, grab him, and say, "Let's go, big boy. (Of course, you have lots of his favorite perfume on.)"**

*Arouse Him Again and Again and . . .*

We asked and we received: After love-making, what should a woman do to arouse you again?

| | |
|---|---|
| Perform oral sex | 61% |
| Kiss and suck a man's nipples | 24% |
| Caress and stroke his body | 10% |
| Masturbate herself | 5% |

As you can see, more than half would like a woman who is adept at oral sex. More than that, they would like her to enjoy it and allow herself to be pleased in the same way.

**I wish women were more open to oral sex—for both parties. Don't be afraid to let a man explore your body with his tongue, and don't be afraid to stimulate him in the same way.**

**A woman adept at oral sex is a sought-after being. All the crude jokes about men wanting a girl who can suck chrome off a bumper have a lot of hidden significance.**

**After lovemaking a woman can arouse me again by holding me, talking to me, and kissing me all over, especially my penis.**

**It's a very special feeling to have a woman go down on you lovingly and enthusiastically, knowing she likes what she's doing.**

Don't shy away from oral sex—80 per cent of all men enjoy it. Some find it equally or more satisfying than normal fornication. Don't be afraid; it won't hurt if both of you want it.

I'm most turned on by a lady who takes a few minutes to freshen up a bit (as I like to do myself), and then in a sexy way suggest that I perform oral sex on her or vice versa. I like seconds, so to speak, but not sloppy seconds.

Enjoy oral sex. As long as the man is clean, it feels good and it can't hurt.

Lightly stroking my thighs and my penis while kissing and nibbling on my ear and neck. Also rubbing her body against mine feels good.

Lie with her head on my chest or shoulder and fondle my penis, while talking about fantasies and love.

Sit up on top of me so I can look up at her and fondle her breasts.

I realize that my wife is a rare find, but I also believe more women have the ability to be better at oral sex than they are. My wife is truly devoted to fellatio, and we both enjoy it.

Another great turn-on for arousing a man is kissing and sucking his nipples. "Just like women, we love to have our nipples kissed and caressed," wrote a Florida hotel manager.

Slowly start exploring my body, first with your fingertips and then with light licks and kisses. Erotic areas for me include nipples, face, and inner thighs.

Some gentle nipple nibbles and caresses is the quickest recharge I know. Some genital kisses and licking works beautifully, too.

If a woman wants to arouse me again, she should kiss me softly and rub my chest. Then I like her to start kissing and sucking my nipples, while gently fondling my penis and thighs.

Attention to my nipples, especially oral attention, never fails to arouse me.

If neither of these methods tempts you, here are other suggestions:

- "Nibble on my ear or stroke my chest, working downward into the groin and the inside of my thighs."

81

- **"Get scantily dressed in sexy clothes (a transparent nightgown and high-heel shoes)."**
- **"She should let me kiss her feet."**
- **"Do a striptease."**
- **"Don't let me go to sleep."**
- **"Watch an X-rated movie with me."**
- **"Tell me how much you love me and need me, and that you can't do without my body."**

Then there are some men who don't need help at all. A fifty-six-year-old lawyer from Virginia wrote: **"Nothing helps, I'm always aroused!"**

*Plan More Time for Lovemaking*

Our schedules are programmed around work, children, household chores, but they don't include time for sex. **"Women should make lovemaking more of a priority; allow more time for it"** was a comment repeated often. (It sounded more like wishful thinking than a reproach.) To make love, to feel inspired, to be able to relax and enjoy it, you need time.

Before you wail about your work load and all the demands on your time, rest assured that the laundry, or any other chore you have to do, won't run away. Give yourself a break, enjoy your man instead. A lot of men complain that their woman doesn't give them the time and attention they'd like.

What we do, and even how well we do it, is a question of priorities. When we feel that something is important, we always find time for it. Isn't sex important anymore? Isn't this a sign of how things have changed since you first met him? Wasn't that a time when sex took first place? Nothing else mattered! Why then do we allow it to become less important than the laundry or a visit to a friend?

Suggestions like the following, which comes from a surgeon in San Francisco, could help you to break out of a rigid schedule:

> **As a minimum, set aside one to two hours a week for a tryst with him only; arrange for an intimate night away together every six to eight weeks. Use imagination in setting things up for your evening of intimacy. When the circumstances allow it, dress up for him, model, do a striptease, playact the role you both enjoy, act out fantasies. Most important, on those special occasions pretend you're a $1,000-a-night whore and set about to earn your money plus a bonus.**

Maybe not everybody wants to go so far as "earning a bonus," but making time for these special moments will show him that he is still a priority for you.

*Allow Him a Quickie Now and Then*

This advice sounds like the opposite of what you just read. Yes, it is, but then again it isn't. Sometimes you don't have time to indulge in extensive foreplay or sensuous lovemaking—say, when you have to be at the office at nine and it's now 7:45. But his sexual urge doesn't recognize that, and even a promise for a romantic evening won't take care of his erection at this moment.

Are you saying that he should understand that you have to get to work? He does, but since a bit of your time is all that's needed, give him ten minutes and keep him from being frustrated all day.

A quickie can make a difference in everyone's life, as the following story shows:

> Our love life had come to a standstill because of our different work schedules. I worked until 1:30 P.M. and came home around two, while the children arrived from school between two-thirty and three o'clock. My wife, Emma, worked evenings. So there was little time to make love, short of going away for a weekend, which we couldn't afford. Occasionally I had tried to use the time between my

arrival—half an hour at the most— and that of the kids. Emma objected because she felt that she was just being used for sex.

When the situation had deteriorated so much that it affected our life together, Emma went for help. Now she has sex with me whenever we get a chance. And she recently told me that she enjoys the quickies, too.

Lack of time is one reason for intense, short lovemaking, but men like it for other reasons as well. **"A quickie has a touch of frivolity, of blatant sex** (turn-ons at any time), **and it provides a change of pace."**

So the next time, instead of saying, "Not now, we don't have time," use this as another way to combine your sexual power with his pleasure.

### Don't Fake It

Should you fake an orgasm? No! **"I prefer when the woman I make love to is honest, and tells me when she didn't have an orgasm. It gives me the chance to satisfy her, and I feel she cares for me enough to share her true feelings."** This encouraging viewpoint is that of a twenty-five-year-old pilot.

An attorney in Indiana, writes:

**A woman should be as responsive
to what the man is giving (and let
him know she likes it) as he should
be to her. Men have as great a need
to give as to take. This includes
saying no in a definite way rather
than faking it. If she doesn't want
to sleep with the man and just pre-
tends, it may kill future enjoyment
for both."**

The notion that if you don't have an orgasm during intercourse you're not a real
woman or your man is a bad lover is slowly
disappearing. Most women today know that
they needn't be ashamed if they make love
without reaching a climax. If they really want
help, they can certainly get it: **"I love it when
a woman shows me how I can satisfy her. It
makes me feel needed and brings me very
close to her."**

By asking for a man's help, you flatter him.
He will be happy that he can do something
for you, and he'll oblige. But if you pretend—
and a man who knows his woman well can
tell when she does—he will feel hurt by your
lack of trust.

Sometimes you won't have an orgasm, even
with his help. Maybe you are tired, maybe
you just don't feel like it. But instead of faking, reassure him. A banker from Toledo
wrote:

**There are times when my wife doesn't have an orgasm when we make love, but I don't feel bad about it, because she always tells me, "Honey, just having you inside me feels good." It brings me very close to her, and I always try harder to please her the next time. I suppose I am grateful that she allows me pleasure without asking anything in return.**

Whatever the reason, we aren't machines and we can't be expected to do things the same way every time, so it's best to be open and honest. He will understand. After all, sometimes he doesn't feel like making love, or needs your help to have an orgasm.

*Don't Make Him Feel Guilty about His Desires*
If you can show a man that you're comfortable with his sexuality and that you understand his needs, you will have a devoted mate. After the thousands of letters I've read, I'm certain that putting a man at ease sexually is the most important ingredient for a happy relationship. I was once present when one woman made a whole roomful of men and women feel at ease about sex. Shere Hite was the guest speaker at a breakfast meeting, and the audience of about forty-five men and fifteen women were all dressed in conserva-

tive business suits, ready to go to work after the talk.

Hite started her speech by asking: "What do you think of the clitoris?" Nobody had an answer. In fact, these business persons looked petrified. She continued on the subject for half an hour, and by then the audience had come back to life. The relaxed way she spoke about sex proved how comfortable she felt both with her own sexuality and with that of the men and women she was addressing. When she had finished, the admiration for her was obvious. Some of the men asked questions, and many went up to her to shake her hand. The understanding and openness she showed made the members of her audience, who were shocked at first, feel at ease. They knew, especially the men, that this woman understood them, and was equally as interested in sex as they were.

Once you convince a man that you share his outlook on sex, he will never be afraid that you will make him feel guilty about his needs. What makes a man feel guilty? Here are some remarks of our survey respondents:

- **"What, again? Are you a sex maniac?"**
- **"Let's hurry, I don't think we should be doing this."**
- **"I don't think we should tonight— anyway it's a sin."**
- **"Hurry up, you take too long."**

- "Are you done?"
- "No, we've already made love twice this week."
- "What, again, you just had it last night."
- "Are you still horny?"
- "You'll get my clothes dirty."
- "We might stain the sheet."
- "I once had a relationship with a woman who occasionally masturbated me to orgasm, and then after I came she complained that there was 'stuff' all over her hand. I felt embarrassed— as if I should be ashamed that my cock and sperm are part of me."

Women who react like this seem to think that men have a disease, not a desire. Comments such as those above imply something is wrong with the person, and therefore will lead to feelings of shame and guilt.

A woman does not always have to say yes, but whatever you say, never make a man feel ashamed for wanting you.

## CHAPTER FIVE

# Indulging Yourself Sexually

At first glance this might appear to be a self-ish attitude, but the comments from the survey respondents indicate that it is the biggest thrill a woman can give a man.

It's very important that the woman enjoys herself. First by being comfortable with me, then by doing whatever she needs to fulfill herself.

Her pleasure is always more important than mine.

A woman should not be afraid to please herself, because that pleases me.

The most exciting women I have made love to were able to convey to me what they needed to come and that what I was

**doing felt good. Her excitement would heighten my own.**

Knowing that he is causing your pleasure makes him feel important, needed, maybe even indispensable. As you can see, pleasing yourself is in no way selfish, but a goal that will help you both enjoy lovemaking even more.

If you still doubt that pleasing yourself is one of the most important ingredients for good sex, think of other situations in life and ask yourself this question: When are you the happiest? Isn't it when you have done something exactly as you wanted? When things went your way? When you *participated* fully?

It's the same when you make love. You should always know what you're doing and, more important, *why*! If you have sex with your man because you feel like it, or because you want to please him, remember that the decision is yours. Being aware of this freedom of choice will have a positive effect on your enjoyment.

However, some women are held back or intimidated by their backgrounds or upbringing. They were taught different values, which are difficult to shake off even when they have lost their validity. But if you want to be in control of your sex life as well as other situations, nothing will stop you from finding out what to do.

*Accept Sex as a Natural Part of Life—Get in Touch With Your Body*

One of the main differences between women and men is that they don't perceive sex the same way. For a woman sex is usually linked with emotions and sentimental feelings. For a man it is usually seen as a natural function, taken in stride like other needs of the body, and this attitude makes him less vulnerable emotionally. Because of this, men don't understand why women aren't as relaxed about it as they are, or why many women can't enjoy sex without an emotional attachment.

**Feel comfortable with yourself and your sexuality. Don't be afraid to be open with your lover. Share your fears and desires with him, like yourself and your femininity.**

**Women are generally excellent at expressing their emotions. However, they should be more secure about their sexuality.**

Whether this different outlook results from upbringing or social standards is not really the issue. Here we are concerned with how the two viewpoints can be brought closer together, not just in order to please the man, but also to achieve a mental unity that is the foundation for any mutual enjoyment, especially sex.

Therefore, women must understand that

sex is a human need that cannot always and only be connected to emotions, but may be enjoyed on its simplest level—a physical pleasure.

An accountant from Oklahoma summed it up this way: **"Take sex less seriously and have more fun."** Here's what others said:

**Relax. Allow your sex life the same privilege you give to your everyday life. Don't deny yourself the pleasure. Let the sensation occur.**

**Sex is an enormous pleasure allowed to everyone. It is the joy that you can truly flip out over—so why not? I enjoy sex in all ways: quiet, sensual, soothing, up to and including loud, crazy animalistic sex. I don't feel guilty or embarrassed by any form, and I love to have sex with a woman who feels the same.**

**Love your body. Sex is difficult with someone who's ashamed of herself or doesn't know her body's reactions.**

Accepting sex as a natural part of life also means knowing your body; knowing how you react sexually and what feels good where. How else can you tell your partner what to do?

I would suggest a woman should get to know her own body, both physically and psychologically. Then she can enjoy the pleasures of lovemaking. For example, know just how to create friction on her clitoris so that pleasure results. Know how to be in touch with the feelings when this plateau is reached. Then responding naturally and without hesitation will heighten her pleasure.

Most sex therapists believe that masturbation is a good way to get acquainted with yourself, but before you do that, learn about your body and its sexual signals. Don't be afraid to look at yourself. Stand in front of a mirror nude and examine yourself. Many a woman will be surprised to see what a nice body she has; her breasts may be every bit as beautiful as those of a *Penthouse* centerfold. If you find yourself overweight, remember that you don't need to be as skinny as a model.

The next step in getting in touch with your body is to pay more attention to the sensual part of your personality. Acknowledge the things around you that make you feel romantic or excite you. Since stimulation is an individual matter, these range from hearing music to wearing silky underwear to running through a field on a sunny afternoon. Take the advice of this archaeologist from Philadelphia: **"Feel** your sexuality. Live your sexuality twenty-four hours a day. Never think of yourself as an ordinary woman. Always be aware of how many men you will attract with your attitude, style, and apparel. Think of yourself as the most sensual and vibrant woman in existence!"

Following these steps will help focus how you feel about sex, and how much you want it or need it. It will also make it part of your everyday life, and not something that you do only in the dark behind closed doors. This does not mean that you make love with anybody, anywhere, anytime. But being aware of your sexuality and accepting it will allow you to choose the best way to fulfill it and, more important, to enjoy it.

### Don't Preoccupy Yourself with What He Might Think

It's dangerous to jump to conclusions. How can you possibly imagine what a man thinks about you? Assuming that he might think this or that could spoil things for both of you, and prevent you from doing something you really want to do.

Most men don't judge a woman for what she does, but rather how she does it. If you really feel like going to bed with someone right away, do it—and don't worry about what he thinks. If he likes you, he'll be delighted. If he doesn't, sleeping with him right away won't change anything, but in the meantime you'll have gotten what you wanted.

Worrying about what a man will think of you can result in confusion. A stockbroker in Chicago wrote:

> **Today it is difficult to do something right. When I ask a woman to go to bed with me on the first date, I get answers like "What do you take me for?" And if I don't ask and let the relationship stay platonic for a while, the woman will ask, "What's matter with me, don't you like me?"**

A lot of men feel confused about how to deal with women, so instead of prolonging a situation in which two people are hesitant, give him a helping hand and start pleasing yourself.

This also works in reverse, by the way. If you don't want to sleep with him right away, say so gently. Explain why, don't just push him away. Remember that egos are fragile. And never sleep with a man because you think he won't be around otherwise. If he really likes you, he'll be there.

*Express Your Desires and Dislikes*

One survey question was: Does it excite you when a woman asks you to touch her?

Yes      93%
No        7%

Women should express themselves better to their partner. Ask them to touch her or to do whatever else pleases her—because an unexpressed urge or desire that is not satisfied will result in frustration. I have tried to bring this out in several of the women I have had relationships with, and they have expressed their gratitude because it has helped them in their other relationships or marriage.

Don't be afraid to be a woman. Get in touch with your emotions and follow through with them. Just being there and not sharing the experience will damage the relationship in the long run.

Don't be afraid to say yes if you want it. Good sex, and I mean really good, is a mutual act, and anything less than that is just an extended form of masturbation.

Talk to your partner before, during, and after making love. Tell him what you like, really stress what you like, no matter how simple it may seem to you.

Let your man know during lovemaking just where you're at! What turns me on more than anything else is when I know that my partner is satisfied and enjoying it as much as I am.

Don't make your lover try everything he knows in the hope that he may hit on what you like—he may not have much of a repertoire. Then what?

A woman must communicate with her lover. She shouldn't be afraid to tell him to kiss her here or there, or to touch her this way or that way. Every woman is different, and what pleases one might not please the next. Show your lover what is best for you.

Every woman responds differently. I am a better lover when I know what does or doesn't work. I usually ask, but I do not always know when I get too rough or, for that matter, when I do the one thing which drives her wild.

Feedback is the detonator to many a hunk of dynamite.

Just as important as telling a man what you like is telling him what you *don't* like. The only person who can give him that information is you. Advice on this point was straightforward:

Talk, tell us what you want—during, not after, lovemaking!

Don't be afraid to coach your partner in lovemaking. You know your body better than he does, and you know what does or doesn't turn you on. Gentle guidance, either verbal or with your hands, will be accepted gladly by your lover.

Don't be afraid to say no if the time isn't right.

Instead of being horrified when your man asks you to make love in a position you don't care for, just say so. Don't make the poor guy feel so guilty.

Obviously, expressing our dislikes is as much part of a fulfilled sex life as expressing our desires. But one word of warning: Whatever you say, say it kindly. Here is an appeal from an executive in Cleveland: **"Be more aware of the fragile ego when you reject us!"**

*Be Less Self-Conscious—Enjoy Your Sexuality*
"Let yourself go. Get turned on to your body. Tune in to your feelings—sex is fun. Enjoy!" This was the comment of a forty-three-year-old college professor from Canada. Similar thoughts along this line are:

A woman shouldn't worry only about pleasing a man, but more about pleasing herself. If she does that, it will be more enjoyable for both partners. When the woman is pleased, so is the man.

Lose your inhibitions. Speak your mind about love and do what pleases you.

Be a bit of an exhibitionist. Feel free about your body.

A woman should be proud of her figure no matter what it's like.

Let yourself go and do what comes naturally. Don't fake anything.

Don't let inhibitions or conventions prevent you from being open enough to experiment with your pleasure through a variety of kisses, caresses, and positions.

Don't play games with your desires—do it because you want to.

If we need any more encouragement than this, we're in trouble! It's heartwarming—or, to be less sentimental, exciting—to hear in so many words that our pleasure is what comes first. Why then are we so afraid to go for it? Maybe because we aren't aware of our needs as we should be.

I would like women in general to be more in touch with their own sexuality and needs, and not be afraid to ask, in a loving way, for what they want. I personally feel that whatever turns her on pleasures me. Seeing her feel good makes me feel good. What goes around, comes around.

Before being accused of overemphasizing *our* pleasure, let me clarify: Being aware of your sexuality does not mean that you have to know the best way to have the most orgasms. Much of what we hear and read about sex today gives the impression that quantity is what counts most. Too much emphasis is put on how to do it "right."

There is no such thing as doing it right or wrong, because what pleases one person may be wrong for another. This is not to say that you can't improve, but in the end every person has to make love in his or her own special way.

Don't compare yourself with others. Do what's best for you and your partner. Love-making is not a competitive sport, but a private and personal way to share.

Learn more about yourself. Find out what you enjoy and what makes you feel relaxed. I have found some women to be somewhat tense. This complicates things for both of us.

Admit, at least to yourself, that you get horny, and don't act prudish.

Don't be afraid of sex.

Enjoy your own body more.

Get in touch with yourself, realize that you enjoy and want good sex.

Dare to be.

*Indulge Your Fantasies*

Once you're aware of the things that stimulate your sexual desires, you won't think it wrong to let your imagination run away with you when you see a terrific hunk of a man across the room. In fact, the fantasy might make the dream come true: By making you appear more available, it could encourage him to approach you. A student from Massachusetts commented:

Why be so aloof? Why act in such a standoffish way? When a meeting, chance or otherwise, occurs, why only fantasize about the man and his abilities? And when you decide to enjoy the fellow, let your hair down

**and talk freely about your likes and fantasies. If you encourage the man to reciprocate, a very satisfactory relationship can develop.**

Fantasies also help put you in the right frame of mind. With the busy and varied lives women lead today, it's sometimes difficult to be in the mood at the same time your partner is. Some days you would rather curl up with a book than make love—not because you're not interested, but simply because nothing has stimulated you enough. Picking up some erotic reading or creating your own scenes and characters can achieve miracles in no time. All that is needed is to let your body do what your mind dictates.

Fantasies are an important part of keeping our sex lives interesting—where would masturbation be without them?

**Exchange your fantasies and don't be afraid to play them out.**

**Be a lady of the Eighties. Be bold and help your man to satisfy your desires and fantasies.**

*Show Him What Feels Good*

**"Be more specific. Hints are often hard to understand."** Or, as a California lawyer put it: **"Show your lust. Don't just expose your body, let us see your soul."**

Communication in sex is as important as in other aspects of our daily life. It means telling your partner specifically and explicitly what you want and need. **"I'll do just about anything a woman desires of me sexually, but I don't like trying a dozen things that turn her off in order to find one thing that she especially likes. Keep the guessing games on television and out of the bedroom."** This is an important message. Even when you're with a man who wants to please you, you have to let him know what feels good. If you don't, he may end up doing just what you don't like.

A young accountant from San Jose wrote as follows:

> **Never be afraid to show a man what you want and what really turns you on. Some men, including myself, will go out of their way to please and satisfy a lady emotionally and sexually. But sometimes there can be some misconceptions as to what she really wants, and there's no way to find out unless she shows me.**

An architectural draftsman from Milwaukee put it this way: **"I like my partner to be talkative and give encouragement, to show** me what she wants and then to let me know when I'm doing it right."

If verbalizing what you want isn't easy for you, start by encouraging him when he does something you like. Tell him, "Oh, I like that." "Keep it up, it feels good. "You do that so well, do it again." Another way to express your delight is by moaning softly. Once you're comfortable about showing your pleasure in this way, it won't be too difficult to say: **"Please kiss my nipples."**

**I feel more aroused when my partner is obviously excited. Sighs, moans, and words of approval or requests for more of whatever I'm doing therefore, get me going.**

**I like when a woman shows me what she needs. I really love communication during sex play. It needn't be verbal—she may push my face down between her legs, or simply unzip her pants, or do something as subtle as licking between my fingers.**

With some men, however, more than a hint is needed. When you want him to touch your clitoris, don't just put his hand there. Guide him to show him the rhythm and speed you like, and he'll soon catch on. As sex therapists Masters and Johnson put it: "Neither partner can have an orgasm for the other. They can only help each other."

"I like a partner who shows me what she wants. The less time I spend finding out her pleasure, the more time I can spend pleasing her," a newspaper reporter from Indianapolis agrees.

"I appreciate if a woman shows me what to do, because pleasing her is as important to me as my own pleasure, perhaps more. Without this communication I'm a little uncertain of my performance."

*Don't Feel Inadequate—Speak Up*

Women who cannot have an orgasm often regard this as a deficiency on their part. They feel that it's their fault, or, worse yet, that there is something wrong with them. These negative feelings can lessen a woman's interest in sex, and increase her anxiety during lovemaking, which prevents her from having an orgasm every time. In most cases, the problem results from a lack of communication and unexpressed desires. Unfortunately, women with this difficulty are not aware of its cause, and keep blaming themselves.

Here is testimony from a husband:

> My wife could only have an orgasm when she was on top of me, but since she felt that this was not normal, she hesitated to tell me. As a result, she rarely reached a climax—a situation that I interpreted as a lack of love.

**Finally she went to a marriage counselor. After only a few sessions she understood that she was not abnormal, but simply needed to communicate her feelings to me. Now she feels free to enjoy sex the way it is best for her, and we both achieve sexual fulfillment.**

As this case shows, we women need to be more demanding when it comes to our own pleasure. Here is a suggestion from a doctor in Nevada: **"Initiate sex, be the active partner. Emphasize your own orgasm before the man's."**

Most people believe that men reach orgasm quicker than women. Studies done by Alfred Kinsey, however, showed that a woman can reach a climax equally fast once she is stimulated enough. How much is enough? This question has to be answered individually, but fortunately men understand and acknowledge this. And a sales representative from Seattle wrote: **"Every woman is different and what it takes to please one might not be right for another. So let your lover know what's best for you to get an orgasm."**

Revealing what turns you on will come easy once you understand that in the eyes of a man, **"Nothing that pleases two lovers can be wrong."**

## CHAPTER SIX

# Indulging Your Man Sexually

After stressing the importance of women's sexual desires, especially the knowledge that our enjoyment is what pleases and excites our partners most, let us now turn to men's sexual needs.

A man's need for sexual satisfaction is not necessarily greater than a woman's; sexual appetites vary among men as well as women. But since men tend to look at sex as a natural function and do follow their desires more readily than women, it often seems that way. When a man sees a woman who appeals to him, he doesn't block the desire he feels at that moment. Instead he yields to it (though he doesn't necessarily chase her down the street!). When a picture, a scent, a remark stimulates him sexually, he welcomes and enjoys it. This readiness is often misinterpreted to mean that a man's sexual needs are greater or that sex is all he wants.

How well a woman understands this delicate balance of real sexual need and readiness can determine the success of a relationship. For example, an intelligent awareness prevents her from being jealous, for she will realize that the stimulation her partner feels when looking at another woman does not indicate a lack of love for her. She will understand that his desire to make love to her four times a week (or more) doesn't mean that he sees her only as a sex object.

As we have seen, satisfying a man sexually has to be combined with other elements, such as affection, honesty, and understanding. It is up to us to find out how much of each our partners need. Women are good at this—usually better than men—and we should make use of our talents in supplying our men with the right amount of sex and emotional support.

*Discuss Sex with Your Man—Outside the Bedroom*

The grievances you have about your sex life should not be discussed while making love. Criticism at this time is hurtful and does not fall on an understanding ear. Instead, choose a time when you are neither angry nor upset—and no longer in the bedroom. Here's a suggestion from a salesman in St. Paul:

**I think that both partners should tell each other—outside the bedroom—**

**what feels good and what doesn't, and make suggestions about what to do differently next time. With the emotions and ego out of the way, a man will listen to you and see your point more objectively.**

Talking about sex is not easy for many of us, but when we get comfortable with the subject, communicating our feelings lays the groundwork for what happens in the bedroom. You might start by talking about an arousing book or movie. Tell him why you found it exciting, and ask him how it affected him. Another way to talk about sex is to refer to the last time you made love. Give him a compliment, emphasize how much you enjoyed it, and tell him that you're looking forward to the next time.

**Sex is a healthy and desirous part of life, and women should not be embarrassed or avoid the subject of sex outside the bedroom. It's then that they should be suggestive and playful about it.**

**I think a couple should talk about sex. If your partner did something you liked or didn't like, discuss it outside the bedroom. It will make for a better time in bed and probably a better person out of you.**

It is important to tell your partner—after sex, out of bed—what was best or not.

Speaking about sex is important. It allows us to share our experience and feelings.

Openness can also prevent us from staying in unhappy relationships too long. A twenty-nine-year-old machinist from North Carolina gave this advice: **"If a woman is not satisfied with what she's getting sexually, she should speak to her man about it. If it turns out that they're not sexually compatible, they should call it quits and find other partners."**

*Take the Initiative*
**"I get tired of being responsible for initiating a mutual activity"** was the comment of a forty-eight-year-old salesman from New York State. A Dentist in Delaware reiterates the same point:

> I get very tired of always providing the initative for sex. If a woman has little initiative, over time you get the impression that sex is an imposition or a due to be paid. If she's hungry, she asks to go out for dinner. If she's horny, she should let her man know she wants it. It's more fun to deliver a needed item than to deliver an item that is merely accepted.

Others agreed:

Be the one to initiate sex more often. I once let a relationship lapse just because I was tired of always being the one to start our lovemaking.

Don't be a dead fish, use more initiative.

Don't expect the man to do everything.

Men also like to be made love to. When you're together, touch him first sometimes. Go to bed with him and don't wait to see what he'll do. This flatters him and will greatly arouse him.

Be more active in bed. In these sexually liberated times, women let themselves be picked up as often as men pick them up. But all too often it stops there. In bed she gets made love to, not with. The initiative stops after she says, "I find you very handsome and I want to go to bed with you." I'm not saying this is bad; what I'm saying is go for it! Take the lead. You know what you want and you can have it. No man worth his salt is going to say no. Don't be afraid to do what you want.

Being the initiator will bring us both pleasure. How otherwise can I learn something? It shows me she is open and confident,

**which means I found a woman and not some shallow mouse—whew!**

**I like it when a lady takes the initiative sometimes because it puts excitement and variety into the relationship.**

These pleas for action don't indicate perpetual erections. Sometimes men too need to be stimulated in order to want sex. They like playing the passive role, being the object of female desires—at least part of the time. As one man put it: **"Don't always look at men as the stronger sex, we're not."**

Comments like these also show that infrequent sex doesn't necessarily mean that a man loves her less. It probably means that he needs help. Rather than feel unloved, take matters into your own hands, and initiate lovemaking. It doesn't have to become the rule, but on days when his libido is low, become the aggressor. As one man wrote, **"It's always a thrill to know she wants it."**

*Let Your Appearance Give Way to Passion*
Whoever has taken the initiative in lovemaking, relax and enjoy the fun. Don't worry about the way you look or what happens to your clothing. The survey responses clearly showed that many women are really uptight about what happens to their appearance during lovemaking. So much so that it actually

113

interferes with the enjoyment of it. **"Don't mess up my makeup!"** is a frequent request. But how can you make love, let alone enjoy sex, without smearing your makeup?

**"Don't wrinkle my blouse"** and **"Don't mess up my hair"** are the two worst offenders—all men seem to have heard them at one time or another. The women who make these requests certainly can explain why their blouses or hairdos should be protected, but when all is said and done, remarks like these convey one of two things: either a lack of interest in your partner (otherwise, your blouse wouldn't be more important than the man), or a wish not to make love at all. **"With my ex-girlfriend all I heard when we went to bed was watch my hair, don't mess up my clothes."** It was such a put-off that most of the time I didn't make love to her,"** remarked a Boston law student. A Chicago accountant criticized the complaint, "You're messing up my hair," with this comment: "Gee whiz, I mean we're going to make love and you're worried about your *hair*?"

Another told this story:

> My last girlfriend became increasingly concerned about her appearance, such as her hair and makeup. After sex she would often sit up in bed nude with a compact and check her lipstick, makeup, and hair. I got turned on just watching her and

**would start kissing her shoulders, back, or neck, but she would say "I'm busy now" or "You just had some."**

Looking at it from a woman's point of view, there are times when you don't like having your hair messed up—just after a visit to the hairdresser, for example. It seems like such a waste. But is it really? A hairdo can always be redone, a blouse can always be ironed, but an adventure or a few hours of pleasure can never be recaptured. Once you've missed them, they're lost forever.

*Who Should Undress Who?*

Do you like to be undressed by a woman?

The answers to this question were surprising, yet very informative. A total of 86 percent of the respondents wanted to be undressed by a woman. No, not just the shirt and tie. **"I love it when she undresses me completely"** is what they like best.

**"Being undressed by a woman is a very sensual experience that manifests caring and is really a part of good lovemaking"** is how a purchasing agent from Idaho sees it. Here is what an engineer on the Mississippi River wrote: **"I can usually tell what a woman is going to be like in bed when she starts to undress me. If she takes her time and teases me as she goes along, then I know she likes**

to fool around a lot before the lovemaking part. If she strips me down, I get the impression that she wants something in a hurry."

"I do enjoy being undressed by a woman because this shows me that she is interested in making me feel attractive and important," remarks an advertising executive in New York City.

> I love when a woman undresses me. You learn a lot about women that way. It's silent language at its best!

> I like to be undressed by a lover—except for awkward things like pulling my pants over my thighs or a pullover over my head. I also like stripping for a woman. I get very excited when she just watches me.

> Yes, I do like to be completely undressed by my partner, especially after having watched her disrobe in front of me.

Of course, men would like to return the favor by undressing their woman during foreplay:

> Undressing a woman very slowly, piece by piece, I can enjoy looking at her in various stages of nudity.

> I like it slowly, sensually, during fore-play. Exploring with caresses and kisses all

parts of her body as her skin becomes exposed, there is no rush! Sometimes there is an incredible sensuality in the way a woman arches her back to allow you to slip off her panties.

Undressing a woman gives me a chance to kiss and make love to every part of her body, preparing her for what is to come.

There seems to be no way to sensually remove a woman's pants. But unbuttoning a blouse with her arms around my neck is thrilling. Pulling her panties off with her hands in my hair is the maximum.

Undressing a woman is a sensual experience to be relished and to be done with care and finesse.

Yet only 55 percent want their woman totally naked while making love. Some 20 percent said they liked women sometimes nude and sometimes, for a change of pace, partially dressed. And 25 percent prefer a woman to wear sexy, scanty lingerie all the time.

Nudity is nice, but semi-nudity is nicer! A man knows what's beneath a woman's panties or bra, but it's his imagination that sets his blood at white heat. Getting a glimpse at what he's not to see . . .

I find a woman partially clothed much more alluring and sexy than completely naked.

Generally I prefer my woman naked with some small jewelry items, i.e., earrings, short necklace, and rings. But I do occasionally enjoy making love to a woman in a sexy teddy, garter belt and stockings, or crotchless underwear.

But if you prefer to undress yourself, go ahead. A striptease is enjoyed by most men, providing it is done in a "slooooooooow provocative way."

I prefer to have a woman undress in front of me. It helps to get my penis hard and ready for sex.

A woman stripping seductively in front of me is an incredibly sexy experience— but don't ever do it in private (i.e., in the bathroom). To me this shows me that she is either ashamed of her body, has hang-ups, or is insecure—all very unsexy.

A woman walking around in seductive underwear and undressing herself in front of me drives me wild and makes me as hard as steel.

*Make Yourself Irresistible with Beautiful Lingerie*

"Men are very visually oriented; wear sexy underwear and clothes that he likes."

"Feeling a woman's flesh above her stockings when I start to undress her, or fingering a silky teddy and a lacy bra while taking off her blouse, makes her very alluring, and it tells me that I will get what I came for." That's what sexy underwear means to this thirty-eight-year-old owner of a landscaping firm in North Carolina.

The attention given to clothes worn on the street should be extended to our lingerie. Never underestimate the effect of female flesh exposed nicely and naughtily. Let his eyes have a feast and increase his desire for you by allowing him to admire you visually. The Italians have a proverb that will serve anyone who follows it in good stead: "A woman should always be dressed to make love or to die."

Have you ever unexpectedly met someone with whom you would have liked to make love, but then didn't because you remembered the old bra or unattractive panties you were wearing?

Soft, pretty underwear is an important part in your lovemaking, at least in the beginning. A forty-two-year-old lumberjack from California wrote:

**I'm delighted with the emergence of companies like Victoria's Secret and**

**Night Club, offering clothing that emphasize a woman's body, for people who want to add spice to their sex life. When it comes to sex, I see my wife and women in general as the cake and sexy underwear as the frosting. To put it another way, I see my lover as a gift, and as we all know, gifts must have pretty bows and wrappings. I don't know who said it but they were right—"sexy underwear is clothing meant to conceal that fails beautifully!"**

Today there is a great choice of beautiful, sexy lingerie in all price ranges. But this variety does make it hard at times to know what to buy for those special intimate moments. The survey provides helpful answers.

Which kind of underwear excites you?

| | |
|---|---|
| Tastefully sexy | 39% |
| Garter belts & stockings | 26% |
| Naughty & provocative | 21% |
| No underwear | 13% |
| Pantyhose | 1% |

The item mentioned most often as exciting and provocative is without doubt a garter belt and stockings. It is seen as naughty, daring, and tastefully sexy, making it the most exciting piece of underwear a woman can wear. It was mentioned as the most popular item by 86 percent of the men.

**"My wife wears garter belts and sheer stockings most of the time,"** wrote a Minnesota marketing executive, thirty-nine. **"Stockings are in my opinion the sexiest item a woman can wear, because they are open, feminine, sexy, and alluring. Knowing that my wife has exposed thighs above the top of her hose drives me crazy with lust."**

Other alternatives in order of preference:

- g-string panties
- teddies
- half-cup, lacy bras
- peek-a-boo bras
- crotchless panties
- half slips
- transparent short nightgowns
- anything made of silk or lace
- seductively nude with a satin ribbon around her neck

**The piece of lingerie that stimulates me the most is a short satin slip through which I feel the motions of our bodies.**

**I like underwear that is more dressy than functional. Lace panties and bras, especially white against a tan, and if they are see-through that's even better. Teddies or camisoles are nice, too.**

What color should these items be?

The sexiest color for most men is still black (41%) next is red (27%), then came white (24%). Pink and light blue had equal appeal (4% each), but interestingly enough, most men who liked these two colors were over fifty years of age.

Knowing what excites a man is one thing. Knowing what is a real turn-off can also be helpful, especially since a woman might not find a pair of cotton briefs so ugly. The second part of the question was: What type or types of underwear turn you off?

A retired Air Force colonel from Wyoming responded: **"Turn-offs are panty hose, panty hose, and panty hose!"**

A teacher from Wisconsin made this remark: **"I love women. They are incredible creatures. Nearly everything they do excites and delights me—with the definite exception of wearing panty hose."**

**Panty hose is a real turn-off, so are girdles and heavy bras. I dislike anything that makes it hard to get where my hands want to go.**

**Panty hose is my most intense dislike. I call it a chastity belt.**

**I dislike panty hose—it was invented by some joyless, profit-motivated company. Try**

**to remove pantyhose gracefully during love-making—what a disaster!**

These opinions reflected what 99 percent of the respondents felt to be the biggest turn-off. For one man it goes so deep that he finds panty hose to be a **"killer of love and sexual arousal."**

Maybe if men wore it, too, they would share women's enthusiasm for the comfort panty hose provides, and be more under-standing. But since this is unlikely to happen, you better think twice before putting it on. Ask yourself: "Is this a day of seduction or not?" If it is, get out the garter belt and stockings; nothing will please him more.

Although panty hose is the most disliked piece of underwear, there are others that don't do much for our sex appeal either. In order of dislike:

- cotton briefs (**"Panties that come up to the waist remind me of prudes or old ladies."**)
- large, loose underwear
- padded bras
- full-cup bras
- girdles
- full slips
- flannel nightgowns (**"They are horrors of lovemaking."**)

- plain white underwear (**"Too sterile-looking."**)

Lingerie should be regarded as a second skin. It should be flattering and make you feel feminine. It can also allow you to be sexy in a way your clothes don't. Professional demands often restrict the kind of clothing a woman can wear. If your job prevents you from looking sexy, use underwear to make up for it. Give your man a surprise and a promise through sexy underwear.

*Don't Let the World Interfere with Your Lovemaking*

> **Whether married or single, don't let the rigors of family or career interfere with a good love life. A former lover once summed it up well, "Sex is an adult play. It is an inexpensive enjoyment when you consider anything else costs hundreds of dollars, and is not nearly as rewarding and enjoyable as good romance and sex."**

Closing the bedroom door should be the signal that the outside world no longer exists. All that matters now is your man and making love. To reach this stage of bliss and relaxation, you must keep your daily preoccupations from interfering with and spoiling your mutual fun. Whether you verbalize your preoccupations or not, men are very aware of them and find them distracting.

A twenty-five-year-old veterinarian from Jacksonville explains it this way: **"If a woman is worrying during lovemaking about what she will fix for supper, or tomorrow's exams, I would rather forget the whole thing. Lovemaking is as much mental as physical, and the right mood is essential."**

Others said:

**I get turned off when a woman makes comments which are superfluous to making love. Sex is not merely a physical thing for me.**

**Anything that has nothing to do with what we are doing I find distracting. I actually had a girl once who asked: "Do you believe in God?"**

**Something unrelated to passion and sex breaks my concentration.**

**When you are with a man, make sure you are not somewhere else!**

**Talking about other things than love signifies a lack of attention to me. After all, when I'm in bed with a woman I give her all my attention.**

Your attention and thoughts should include only your man, because **"making love is a time to forget all else."**

*Remarks to Avoid: Before—During—and After Making Love*

A casual remark made at the wrong time by someone we love can be painful. The following comments—all quoted by survey respondents as things they hate to hear before, during, or after lovemaking—should serve as warnings.

### Before

- "Hurry up!" ("I hate to hurry. I like foreplay and lovemaking that's slow and sensuous. And when I'm feeling spontaneous I don't like to hear these comments.")
- "Did you put the cat out?"
- "How many girls have you made love to?"
- "Is the front door locked?"
- "What if someone finds us?"
- "Are you clean?"
- "Wait, let me get the tissues first."
- "Let me shower first."
- "Let me brush my teeth."
- "Do you know what happened today?" ("Yes, I lost my erection.")

- "What kind of a car do you drive, and how much money do you make?"
- "I don't want any commitment with any man."
- "Wait, I have to put my diaphragm in."

*During*

- "I called mom today."
- "Oh, look, my blouse has a stain."
- "Linda had a baby boy."
- "Are we going steady now?"
- "Oh, I forgot to take my pill."
- "Let's go to church tomorrow."
- "Why did you pick me? Do you really care about me?"
- "Let's get this over with."
- "Did you really mean the things you said?"
- "Oh, I'm not using any contraceptive."
- "What a cute thing you have!" ("One of the biggest turn-offs is to have my penis called by other names. I like a woman to use the names by which my body parts are known, such as prick, cock, or penis.")
- "Will you respect me in the morning?" ("This is a sensitive one with me. I always have the temptation to say something like, 'My respect for you hinges more on your ability to make love than limited sexual activity,' but somehow I

never felt that would go over very well.")

- "I'm not going down on you because I've never done that." ("There are ways of expressing things without being so rough and desire-cutting. If a woman doesn't particularly like something, say it in a more indirect and diplomatic way.")

*After*

- "Are you finished yet?" ("Has to be the all-time turn-off.")
- "Was it good?" ("If she has to ask, it wasn't.")
- "Did you come?"
- "I need a cigarette." ("It turns me off when a woman sits up in bed and lights a cigarette the moment we are done making love.")
- "I have to go to the bathroom."
- "Tell me you love me."
- "If after sex for the first time a woman immediately says how much she loves me, having known me only briefly, that's a turn-off."
- "The dogs are in the trash again. Would you go and clean it up now?"
- "You were great, how was I?" ("I hate grades! If you don't know whether your partner enjoyed it, you're not communicating.")

- "I hope I'm not pregnant!" ("After I've cared enough to ask if she was protected.")

*Never Compare Your Man with Past Lovers*

I am offended by comparisons with other men, good or bad.

References to past boyfriends are a letdown.

I don't want to hear about past lovers. I'm only interested in her and me.

Telling me about how much she liked being with someone else, how good he was—implying that I'm not—makes me get up and leave.

Talk about past boyfriends turns me off. I like warm, affectionate conversation about personal dreams and hopes.

If she says, "I once knew this guy who . . ."—I don't want to know who she knew before me. All that matters is us now.

I dislike comparisons. If I do something she doesn't like, or if I don't do something she would like, she should tell me, not degrade me by comparing.

You are better than my husband. Even if it is meant as a compliment, I hate to be reminded of other men she has been with.

The worst thing for me is to be compared to someone else, or to be told how and what someone else did. If I do not satisfy her, then she should either stop or not be with me at all. I get very jealous and do not like to think that while making love I am not the center of her attention.

I do not like a woman to tell me I'm not doing something the way someone else did. During lovemaking I don't want to think about other people at all, but concentrate completely on her pleasure.

Is bringing past lovers into the picture a female characteristic? Maybe not, and if a man did this to us, wouldn't he be criticized for being insensitive? Wouldn't we feel hurt and rejected by the comparison? And wouldn't we hate to know that he still remembers these women at a time like this?

As one man was quoted earlier in this book: "Try to put yourself in your partner's place. Don't do to him what you don't want to have done to you." This advice should be taken seriously. Don't let the memory of past adventures upset the man you are making love to now.

*Practice Makes Perfect*

There is hardly anything in life that we try or are expected to do well at without having had the time or opportunity to practice it. Making love is the exception. We do it, at least at the beginning, without experience. To overcome this lack of know-how, we have to be open-minded and willing to listen to advice. Here is some from a thirty-five-year-old San Francisco advertising man:

> In my opinion, to be a good lover requires practice. Have you ever heard of an all-star athlete, racecar driver, scuba diver, or any other physical or mental performer having reached success without practice? To that end, my suggestion is obvious—practice makes perfect! To clarify my point, let me say this: I'm not an advocate of free love. But I am a firm believer in using the equipment we were born with—our minds and bodies. Anything left unused or not used to a certain capacity tends to deteriorate (especially with age as an added factor). So why not practice lovemaking discriminately, yet openly, with an eye toward ever increasing the quantity and quality? Practice can make perfect!

Many others shared the feeling that making love more often would help women to become more comfortable with their partner, and that knowing what to do would allow them to relax and enjoy sex more. Although acquiring experience was the general advice, this does not imply changing partners frequently. What it does suggest is practice with the man you love—to find out what he likes and share it with him.

The answers to a two-part question in the survey might help you to know where to start. The question was: Do you like a woman to give you a massage?

The replies were overwhelmingly *yes!* **"Having a woman give me a massage is pure heaven!"**

Where?

| | |
|---|---|
| All over | 42% |
| The back | 25% |
| Neck & shoulders | 12% |
| The penis | 8% |
| The buttocks | 7% |
| The chest | 6% |

**"Massages are relaxing and can be very erotic. I like it when a woman starts on my back, then continues all over my body. If she does a good job I fall sleep, but she can wake me up by massaging my penis."**

In Eastern countries massages have always

been part of erotic foreplay and lovemaking, and women there have been taught how to do it, how to relax and stimulate a man through a good rubdown. Maybe we can catch up a little by remembering where to rub!

## CHAPTER SEVEN

# Keeping Your Man from Straying

Other women should not be a threat to you, if all your man wants—and needs—is you. Of course, this means taking care of all his sexual and emotional needs. This is not difficult when you understand and respect him as a person and love him as a man. For a good relationship, you have to ask, "What can I give?" not just "What can I get?"

Depending on the individual, "a man can be a full-time occupation," and some women do choose to make their relationship a career. Others, with goals of their own, divide their time and attention between outside interests and their man—not always easy to manage and impossible without his help.

When you want your man to help you, you have to take the first step by communicating your needs and thoughts so that he knows what you want. In return, you have to be compassionate and attentive, and to give him your support when it's needed. "It takes two to make a pair, and in order to stay a pair they must know each other well" is how a electronic technician from California put it.

This brings us back to the importance of *communication*. Whether you want a weekend trip to the Bahamas or a romantic evening of love, you have to tell him. Over and over men wrote advice to this effect: **"We aren't mind readers. Please tell us what you want."**

James comes to the office on Monday morning, obviously depressed. His coworker Alex, a man in his late forties, asks him how his weekend was. Quite discouraged, he replies: "I've been with Joanne for fifteen years now, and for the life of me I can't remember her birthday. It's not that I don't love her, I just don't remember, something she will never understand or forgive me for." Hearing James's dilemma, and not being the most attentive person himself, Alex remembers gratefully all the little hints Marie gives him every time an occasion he should remember approaches. Obviously Marie is wiser than Joanne. She has assured herself and her man many happy hours, which Joanne has spent in dispute with James.

Many women think that if a man really loves them he should know what they want. Not true. Even love can't turn someone into a clairvoyant. So be realistic and don't set yourself up for a disappointment. For instance, if your man is preoccupied with work or if he is the distracted type, known to forget birthdays and anniversaries, listen to this advice from a banker in Dallas:

> **Don't wonder if your man will remember your birthday this year. Help him out and say: "I thought for my birthday we might go out for dinner." Or, "I'm thinking of giving a little party." Or, "How about if we invite the Meyers for my birthday?" He'll be grateful for the reminder and will thank you by making it a memorable occasion.**

But you might still ask, "Why should it always be me? Why can't he sometimes take the first step?" That's a good question. He might eventually do so, but how long do you want to wait? You could be waiting in vain, watching your relationship deteriorate. Don't take that chance. Appoint yourself the guardian of your relationship. Give him your support, your love, enough sex, and you will most likely have a man who adores you.

*A Sexually Satisfied Man Is Yours*
**"A woman who is not interested in sex must take the responsibility for an unfaithful man."** This serious accusation comes from a thirty-three-year-old salesman in Los Angeles.

Exceptions aside, men don't stray because they don't love their wives or companions, but, as this survey confirmed, because their sexual needs aren't satisfied at home. Even a long-lasting affair with another woman doesn't mean that a man is no longer in love with his companion. What it does mean is that the "other woman" gives him something his companion doesn't.

Here's an example given by a lawyer from Chicago: **"I have casual affairs to get over my frustration. But after having been with one of these women, there is nothing better than going home, putting my slippers on, and sitting down for dinner with my woman and the kids."**

Most men don't really want to run around, and their consciences do bother them, but frustration is more troublesome than a bad conscience.

Following are the replies we got to our question: Are you sexually attracted to other women?

| | |
|---|---|
| Often | 59% |
| Sometimes | 40% |
| Never | 1% |

And more than eighty percent of the respondents confessed that their interest in other women went beyond attraction!

The second part of the question was: Why?

I'm often sexually attracted to other women, because my wife doesn't give me enough and hides her body too often. She has sex with me only to keep me quiet or to fulfill what she thinks is her obligation. If she would let me see her body and would make passionate love with me, I would be less attracted to other women.

Unfortunately, my wife still is (we have been married fifteen years) too uptight and uncomfortable to openly enjoy sex with me.

My woman is prudish, and doesn't fulfill my sexual needs.

I'm often attracted to other women because sex is a forgotten subject with my wife.

My woman is very good in bed, but doesn't want it as often as I, which leads me to stray.

I require sexual satisfaction three or four times a week. My companion only wants to make love once a week. This leaves plenty of room for other possibilities.

A forty-year-old president of a securities investment company offered these suggestions for improving matters:

**Make your man feel desirable. Let him know you enjoy sex as much as he does, and ignore what you've been taught about what good girls do or don't do. I think most women know what will turn a man on, they just don't follow through for fear they'll be breaking the rules—i.e., talking dirty, acting like a hooker, performing fellatio, etc. Don't worry about being a lady in bed.**

Another said:

**My woman does not believe in any form of oral sex. She never plays with any part of my body, and is glad when I'm through. I must add that we don't communicate.**

**Make love to your man even if you don't feel like it. Be gentle, show him a bit of affection, let him have his fun. After all, it doesn't hurt, does it?**

Of course, your man is with you because he loves you, and he is looking forward to having sex anytime he wants it. When he met you, he thought his days of searching were over, that he could now enjoy sex with love. Don't disappoint him, and don't lose him because you're holding back. One of our respondents asked us to remember always:

**"The staying power of the man is in the woman."**

*Don't Let Sex Become Routine—Be the Aggressor Sometimes*

One survey question asked: Is Your sex life:

| | |
|---|---|
| Not enough | 34% |
| Very good | 20% |
| Satisfactory | 17% |
| Routine | 15% |
| Exciting | 14% |

**Our sex life is very good, but not enough. My woman can go for a week without. Perhaps I have a Chinese food attitude about sex. Half an hour later I'm hungry again.**

**Lovemaking should never become predictable. Each time should be an experience— new and different.**

In our daily life we cannot survive without a certain order. Sex, on the other hand, doesn't thrive on too much regularity. It needs stimulation or its magic will disappear. Without it, as one man wrote, **"It will fizzle away"**—and so will your man, as well as your wonderful feeling of fulfillment as a woman.

So far a lot has been said about how to make love, how to please a man and how to please yourself. This advice can be applied as easily to married people as to single ones, but here are some specific hints from married men that will help prevent your relationship and love life from getting dull:

Try to seduce him over and over again in different ways.

Don't just lie there. Get into the act, enjoy it.

Understand that lovemaking can be perfect only when two people are working together to satisfy each other as much as possible. The male is not supposed to just show up and perform like a stud.

Be willing to try some kinky but harmless things, such as different positions. Act out fantasies, see X-rated movies, and go to burlesque shows, where you can see some teasing techniques. Yes, I would go to a male burlesque show with her, too!

Don't always do things the same, don't get in a rut.

Start to touch your man where you would like him to touch you.

Don't hurry through it, take it slow and graceful. Sex is an art that should be performed gently and with much romance.

Make love when you feel like it, not only on Saturday nights. I might not be ready on the same day every week.

Watch for signs that indicate sex could become a routine.

Be more sensual: Try to put a little variety in love so it won't be boring after a number of years. Make your man feel that he's the greatest lover in the world.

It doesn't take much to prevent lovemaking from becoming a routine. Changing the time, the place, or the position can make all the difference.

Be aware of little things in and out of bed. They will make the difference between boredom and excitement.

Allow us to make love spontaneously sometimes.

Try to prevent monotony from creeping into your love life.

I'm thirty-five years old and have been married for six years to a wonderfully talented, intelligent, and beautiful professional woman, but I'm afraid the heat of passion has ebbed somewhat. However, the mental lock we have on one another is most gratifying. We love each other a great deal and are loyal to one another. Our sex life is somewhat routine. I am always the one who initiates sex. She is always willing, but if she would be the aggressor sometimes, it could save our lovemaking from being so routine.

Obviously this couple has it all, or nearly so. It wouldn't be difficult for this lady to make their relationship 100 percent. All she has to do is make the first move now and then. Why? Her man has given us his reason, but let's us hear a few others:

Be more aggressive and willing. Start with different techniques, do more things that you know turn your man on. Show him that you really care, that you like to make love to him, by initiating it.

Take charge of sex once in a while. A man likes to be attacked, you know! Give him a thrill some morning by letting him wake up with you on top of him.

I like women who are eager to take the lead in anything we do sexually, and who suggest and ask for what they like. Sex should be mutually satisfying, and both partners should be equally eager to participate and enjoy.

Don't be afraid to ask for it anytime you want it. Be spontaneous. Use your imagination to do something different. For example, choose new places or pretend you just met in a bar. Anything that will show your man you still want him.

Be the aggressor, try new things. Don't take your lovemaking for granted. Your man may be tired or distracted. Try to awaken his interest by looking sexy, even if you are just sitting around at home. Take the initiative on occasions.

Most women seem to feel that it's a man's responsibility to actually make love. They should practice with him and try to improve their performance. They can read books and magazines, see movies, etc., where professionals show them what they can do to make their lovemaking more exciting. The few good lovers I have found are the ones who have done this.

If you feel shy about reading books or magazines about sex, don't tell anyone. Let it be your secret. Read them when you're alone. Apply what you read, gently and gradually, to your own lovemaking. Once you feel less inhibited, you can read the magazines together. He will admire you for being so open-minded, and your interest in sex will be seen as a sign of love for him. It will bind you closer together and heighten the heat of passion for both of you.

And here the voice of a happy man:

> **I'm divorced and the lady I plan to marry makes me feel like a sexual wonder god sometimes. At odd times and places she will deliberately provoke an erection and sexual excitement, and will receive me with a delightful hunger. Certainly this "home run" situation doesn't exist all the time, but at least several times a month. She really makes me feel that my cock and my sperm are the only things of importance to her in the whole world—I'm hooked and happy!**

*Don't Let the Children Rob You of Your Man*

- **Unfortunately, I can make love only in my bedroom, because I have three children, and they're all over the house.**

- **Privacy is a rare commodity in our house. The children watch television in our bedroom, and come in anytime they want.**

Yes, privacy certainly is a luxury, but it's one you can afford if you really want it. From the above situations, it's obvious that something has to be done before the sex life of these couples is nonexistent. However, the only people who can make it happen are the man and woman themselves. Relatives and friends won't help. On the contrary, once a couple is married, most people—including parents, siblings, and close friends—forget that a husband and wife need time when they can concentrate only on each other.

To keep your lovemaking alive, or restore passion to your relationship, you need privacy, and if it isn't part of your daily life, you have to start by making some changes.

- Teach your children that they must always knock before coming into your bedroom.
- Move the television out of the bedroom. The gain in privacy will make it worthwhile to forego watching TV in bed.
- Don't let family obligations overwhelm you. Be firm and say no when your sister wants to come over on a night when you had planned to spend time with your man alone.

- If distance allows it, ask him to come home sometimes during his lunch hour.
- Ask a neighbor or a family member to stay with the children for a few hours so that you can meet him after work.
- If you can afford it, plan some weekends without the children.
- If possible, send the children to a relative once a week.

Peter's mother was a widow who lived alone, not far from her son and his family. Since she did not work, she had plenty of free time, which she liked to spend with her grandchildren. Whenever she called to ask if she could come over, her daughter-in-law, Jane, did not have the courage to say no. The result was that she was often still there when her son came home, and then stayed for dinner. Afterward he drove her home. When he returned home the evening was nearly over, leaving little time for a private moment with Jane.

One day when she complained about the lack of privacy, Peter looked at her helplessly and asked, "But what do you want me to do? She is my mother."

"I know she is, and I like her, too, but couldn't we bring the children to her place once a week and let them sleep over?"

Not only did this solution give Peter and Jane an evening for themselves, to do whatever they wanted, it also made his mother feel important and wanted instead of feeling like an intruder.

Arranging moments like these will prevent your children and the world from coming between you and your man.

*Make Love—Don't Just Have Sex*

**"The most beautiful feeling in the world is to have sex with someone you love. When the moment of passion is over, the loving starts."**

Married couples or couples committed to their relationship have an initial advantage over singles: They know that they love each other, and don't have to wonder anymore. They don't have to be afraid that sex is all there is because they know better. But they have to be careful to keep it that way. In having sex a couple should always show their love for each other. To help us do so the following advice from the survey respondents might be helpful:

**Don't make your man feel as if you're doing him a big favor by giving it to him.**

**Participate more—make him return the gift you're giving him.**

**A woman should demonstratively want her man—come on to him. Being lovers is**

not a one-way proposition; the responsibility for good sex belongs to both. Problems arise when one feels as if he/she is doing more than the other and is being cheated; this reduces lovemaking to sex.

Women should train themselves to be in the mood more often so that they can make love with their man and not just let them have sex.

A big help to good lovemaking is knowing what excites your man. Maybe his wishes seem a little eccentric to you, but if they're not harmful to either of you, go along with them. Here are two examples:

I find women's feet very sexy. During lovemaking I often lick the bottom of my woman's feet, or between her toes. This excites me no end, and she enjoys the control it gives her over me. The event becomes so intense and passionate that we wear each other out.

I am a well-built male, 46–34–36, who enjoys having his nipples sucked. I was first introduced to this when I was seventeen by an older woman, and have been hooked ever since. My wife has learned to enjoy it too.

Perhaps your man doesn't have any special needs, or could it be that you have not yet discovered them? But if he does, satisfying those needs can only bring you closer.

*Take Good Care of Yourself*

**"I wish my wife would spend more time on herself instead of the kitchen and the household chores."** This rather plaintive comment reflects the attitude of a lot of men. Another common piece of advice is:

**After you have found your mate, don't let yourself go. Pay attention to your looks and body.**

**Whereas I keep myself in good physical shape, my wife has let herself go, as far as weight is concerned. (She's about sixty pounds overweight.) I find myself often attracted to slimmer women.**

**I see many women, especially as they get older, who let their appearance and figure deteriorate. Speaking strictly for myself, I must be both physically and mentally attracted in order to find a woman sexy and attractive. The best personality in the world doesn't help if she's overweight. This is not to imply that just getting older makes women less attractive. I have seen many older women whom I found very exciting.**

I have included these comments to show how conscious men are of the appearance of their partners. This applies to her clothes as well as her figure.

**Men really love a firm, shapely body. Get out there and exercise, don't keep putting it off. You'll feel better about yourself, too.**

**I find clothing and the way they affect a woman's attitude extremely exciting. My wife always wears the same jeans and same type of shirt, with no concern for whether she's attractive to me. She hates to wear skirts or dresses, and her underwear is boring. My attempts to encourage more provocative underwear create fights. So I've more or less given up hope of enjoying the sight of sexy lingerie. My sexual interest has dropped off as a result, and I will be left with fantasies.**

**My woman knows I like her breasts and dresses for me accordingly, but always with taste and class.**

To find out what men think of their women's physical appearance, we asked this question: What do you think your woman could improve on?

| Figure | 36% |
|---|---|
| Clothes | 29% |
| Hair | 14% |
| She is perfect. | 9% |
| Makeup | 8% |
| Manicure | 4% |

And now to the good news: Would you mind if she spent more money on the above? was another questions. *No—she is worth it!* said 92 percent. **"I certainly would not object to her spending more money on clothes, makeup, etc., because I benefit as much as, if not more than, she."**

*Respect His Taste and Dislikes*

If your man doesn't like flat shoes or a certain dress, don't say: "He doesn't like this dress, but I don't care, I love it." Remember when you first met him how much you worried about what to wear every time you had a date? Consider and respect his opinion as you did then. It is still as important.

One man told us: **"Before I ever get serious with a woman, I take her away on a weekend. Not only to make love to her, but to find out whether she puts the top of the toothpaste back. I want to see how considerate she is in little things."**

This may seem small-minded, but isn't it true that little things, like leaving beard stubble all over the bathroom sink year after year, can drive us crazy?

Here another example of how considerate a woman can be:

> My wife, now in her late fifties, has never worn panty hose because she knows that I don't like it. We have been married for over thirty years. I'll admit that wearing garter belts probably isn't the only reason for our marriage's success, but her consideration for my wishes has certainly made a difference.

When you ask your man's advice about your clothing, or any other matter, listen to him. His opinion is still important, and following his wishes can make for better communication and understanding.

The end of this chapter seems like an appropriate time to find out what one happy man sounds like:

> I felt absolutely fantastic the first time she told me I could have sex anytime I wanted. Remarks like this are touching because they show a recognition of my need. We have sex in a variety of positions, and I like sex at least once a day on the aver-

age. When she says no, it's for a good reason. But when she says yes, it's never grudgingly. She always acts as if she wants it, too, and that makes me feel very secure. I love her very much and will never cheat on her because her attitude toward sex and me is one that fulfills me one hundred percent. She is confident of her sexuality and she has class. If all other women were like her, singles bars would be history.

## CHHAPTER EIGHT

# Making Love in the Right Environments

It's clear by now that a change of pace—making love in different ways, letting our imagination take over, being adventurous—are all sought-after qualities, which add variety to our sex lives. It's not only welcomed, but probably necessary to keep the fire burning.

Realizing just how much a change of pace can do for our lovemaking, and to help our imagination, we have to use whatever we can find. Some diversions require more effort than others, but the one we are dealing with here is relatively simple. All that's expected is to change the environment, to take lovemaking out of the bedroom to **"a picnic table in the woods!"** (Actually, there are many other choices, and luckily most of them are more comfortable than a picnic table.)

One survey question was: Besides the bedroom, what is your favorite place(s) to make love? And it had a follow-up, namely: Why do you prefer this place(s)? Surprisingly, the main reason for choosing a location was **"it's so romantic."** Many men assured us, **"We are just as romantic as women."**

A comment from a young man (twenty-eight) in Buffalo can hardly fail to touch every woman's heart: **"My favorite place would be, no doubt, in the comfort of your embrace."** Another man spoke for his partner and himself when he said: **"Wherever the mood catches us—we like spontaneity."** And from a police officer in California:

> **Always making love in the bedroom gets to be boring. Sure, it's the primary place, but the living room floor or couch is a nice change—also, I still want to try the airline washroom! Not bad for a forty-three-year-old, huh? But, seriously, I have a couple of horses and what's really a turn-on is to throw a blanket on the saddle, get a jug of wine, and head out on the trails in the afternoon. Find a shady spot somewhere secluded and take my time making love. Really great! And it seems to turn the girls on, too. Oh, yes, I did it in a drive-in theater the other night (it's been years since the last time) and it was fun.**

Let's now find out where the mood catches other men (in the order of preference), and why.

*In the Bathroom*

**"Sex in the shower is unsurpassed; it's that natural and clean feeling."** After the bedroom, the bathroom was the choice of 85 percent of the survey participants. Even though the reasons vary, the main attraction of the shower is the closeness it brings.

**Making love in a shower is like throwing a large party in a house trailer—no room to move and you keep bumping into things!**

**It turns me on to explore and to be explored. It's very sexy to touch each other everywhere. Showers before sex are a great way to extend foreplay. After sex they're a warm and intimate experience that extends the ecstatic emotions of sex.**

**Yes, I love to be soaped all over, and nothing is more exciting than soaping up a woman's breasts.**

**To feel her smooth, soft, slippery body against mine is ecstasy! You can explore each other's bodies and break all barriers.**

Making love while in the shower is different and quite arousing, because the beat of the water upon my skin stimulates me even more. For this reason I have purchased a shower massage.

I can look at her and touch her and never stop (and we can't hear the phone ring).

The bathroom lends itself to interesting positions.

It brings closeness and I love it when she washes my penis.

The water makes it pure and clean. Nothing is more arousing than the smell and taste of a clean body.

It seems naughty, yet exciting.

I prefer the bathroom because with the kids in the house, it's private and gives the feeling that we are getting it on behind closed doors, like an afternoon affair.

The bathroom is a turn-on, even for those whose facilities are inadequate: "Unfortunately, our tub is too small, and the shower keeps only one person warm. However, give me a big tub or a larger shower and watch out!"

*In the Living Room*

The warm and relaxed atmosphere of a living room nurtures a slower, more romantic way of lovemaking, and provides a change, or, if you just met, a chance to get to know each other. Its two main attractions are a fireplace, which brings out the romantic side of our lovers, and the space that allows for maneuvering:

**My favorite place is in front of the fireplace in the living room. Why? Men can be romantic, too!**

**I like to make love near the fireplace in the living room because I'm a romantic person.**

**On the rug in the living room. The fireplace throws off a nice, warm light on her body, and three is a lot of room to roll around.**

**The heat of the fireplace gives off warmth to boost our passion and enough light to see each other.**

**In front of the fireplace because it's romantic and sexy. On the couch because it's comfortable and a good place for a woman to be on top.**

If your living room lacks a fireplace, there are still other attractions:

**The thick carpets, the extra space, and the firmness of the floor are better for unusual positions.**

**The furniture—recliner, rocking chair, couch —allows for a variety of positions.**

**Sometimes that's as far as you get.**

**In the living room we can watch X-rated movies on the VCR before or during love-making.**

**The living room sofa, either for variety or because we are there, particularly with a new date who is hesitant to go to the bedroom.**

*In the Arms of Mother Nature*
"Making love outdoors makes me feel as if we were Adam and Eve," wrote a twenty-five-year-old Navy man from Virginia Beach. "I like the feeling of freedom it gives me. The sun, moon, and stars, the fresh air, wind, and sound of the waves on the beach all make it an intense and exciting experience."

In addition to the feeling of freedom, some men expressed that they liked a touch of danger:

The outdoors provides an extra sense of excitement because of the risk of being caught.

I find the chance of being observed very stimulating.

Being outdoors pleases my sense of exhibitionism.

Under a tree, with a warm breeze blowing all over my bare skin.

In the woods, in patches of tall ferns by a brook.

Cornfields in the moonlight amid the fireflies and the stars. Our lovemaking feels such a natural part of the cosmos at such times. So right in the overall scheme of things, it's awesome.

In the grass on a warm, sunny afternoon, right before evening with the glow of the sun on our bodies.

In the forest—it makes me feel primitive and as if I don't have a worry in the world. It's just me and my woman, and I don't have to think about anything else but our love.

If you haven't been keen on the outdoors before, these romantic descriptions should tempt you to try it.

Happy memories are the reason for liking some places, for instance: **"I grew up in the country and it was great sneaking out to the haymow and fixing the bales so it was nice and comfortable for lovemaking."**

We may not be Adam and Eve, but it looks as if the outdoors can make this fantasy a reality.


*In a Swimming Pool—on the Beach—on a Boat*

Water is stimulating not only in the bathroom, but outdoors as well. **"Swimming in the nude is a wonderful, free feeling, which can lead to beautiful intercourse."** This comment reflects the experiences or dreams of many men.

**The feel of the water against our bodies and the sensation of the waves are fantastic during lovemaking.**

**In a pool it is easy to hold and move a woman so that sex is good for both of us.**

**Skinny-dipping is one of the greatest, freest, close-to-nature feelings there is. Nothing compares to it. It's exciting and exhilarating. There is nothing dirty or por-**

nographic about it. Its practice and honesty would go a long way to holding many a failing relationship together.

A white, sandy beach is open and exposed, and the sound of the waves is very soothing. The white sand is a symbol of purity and cleanliness, recalling my first love.

The ultimate way to make love is on the deck of my boat while at anchor off the coast of some island in the Bahamas, or while swimming the seas with the salt spraying and the wind whipping our bodies. (Sorry, all answers are anonymous.)

To be on a lake and feel the sway of the boat and to hear the water slapping up against the hull is a real aphrodisiac.

Rocking in the bottom of a small sailboat adds to the sensuality of lovemaking.

What could be better than making love on the deck of my boat on a moonlit night? It's ecstasy!

*In the Kitchen*
What could be the attraction of this particular environment? Maybe the following replies will help us to understand:

I like to be in the kitchen with my woman because she seems helpless. She is busy and has her hands occupied. I can kiss her neck, stroke her, put my arms around her waist, and it makes me feel comfortable and close to her.

It's the old surprise from behind while she's cooking supper. Besides, what else is there to do but make love while you wait for your meal to get done?

It's great in the kitchen because it's kinky and unusual.

I like the kitchen because we spend a lot of our time there, and if I want her then and there, we'll let it happen.

Performing oral sex on the kitchen table is outrageously good.

To make love on the kitchen table is a fantasy I had from childhood on.

I like it because when it happens on the kitchen table, it's always spontaneous.

And in the event he's the cook, like this young man from Alaska, this is what he would like you to do:

"I like to be fondled when I cook dinner for two."

*On the Backseat of a Chevy*
If you don't have a Chevy, it doesn't really matter. Any car or van will do, moving or parked. At the root of this preference are the memories of youth.

In the back of my pickup truck out in the woods, because it reminds me of when I was young and had the best times of my life.

Making love on the backseat of my car brings back memories of my teens.

I spent a lot of time in a car with my girlfriend when I was younger.

It's still exciting because I used to make out in a car as a teenager.

Ah, to be a teenager in the backseat of the old Chevy! When love and sex were one, all-consuming, and all that mattered.

In my VW window van, where the bamboo shades only partially conceal the interior. This provides added excitement, particularly on a downtown street at night, where we can watch the passing crowd, who are oblivious to our endeavors.

A car is a good way to make love and watch a movie at a drive-in.

It allows for positions not otherwise possible.

Doing it while cruising down the highway would be nice.

It can save you when everything else fails. We make love in the car whenever we can't find a motel room.

I know this is an infantile answer, but I have had some very intimate and satisfying lovemaking sessions on the backseats of Chevrolets. Yes, I agree that it's not a very comfortable or romantic atmosphere, but there was one memorable incident when a woman and I tried lovemaking in the front seat of my car in a suburban neighborhood. During our foreplay we kept hitting the horn. Rather than upsetting us, it broke the tension and made us laugh all evening.

*In the Workplace*
"My office is like a home to me, so why shouldn't it serve as a place to make love?" This was the question of an executive from Denver, Colorado. Another observed, "Making love in the office helps me to integrate

**my life."** Still another commented, **"The office at night provides a quiet haven."**

But workplaces are not only stimulating at night. A young stock clerk wrote that he found it **"very exciting to make love between the file cabinets."** Others discovered that the office floor, a desk, and a closet make good playgrounds for sex, and one even mentioned a three-wheeled post office vehicle.

It might sound a little bizarre, but the reason for choosing these places is the same as for liking the outdoors—the chance of discovery, which adds a new dimension and excitement to sex.

> **I always fantasize about making love on a nonworking day at the construction site where I work.**

> **There is something erotic about making love where I work. We have done it in the commander's office, in the warehouse among the boxes, in the shower of the warehouse, in the front office. After a night of sex in the office it's fun to walk by the desk or chair where you made love and see someone sitting there who doesn't know what happened.**

Should you still doubt why the comfort of a bedroom isn't sufficient, read this comment from a twenty-six-year-old business owner from New York State: **"Because I love sex, the more places it's done, the better. Remember why Sir Edmund Hillary climbed Mount Everest? Because it's there. I have made love on the roof of a house and on a giant glacial boulder in the area."**

*Would You Believe an Elevator?*

Probably most of the locations mentioned so far, you've tried or could have thought of yourself. However, many other sites you have never considered or thought of as having a dual purpose are real possibilities for a change of pace:

- **"On a slow elevator going up in an eighty-story building."**
- **"On the stairs, because they offer a wider variety of positions."**
- **"On the Oriente nude beach on St. Martin's."**
- **"On a bar stool, because it lines us up perfectly."**
- **"On a golf course."**
- **"On the washing machine during the spin cycle. The vibrations are tremendous."**
- **"Adult motel rooms because the mirrors, waterbed, and X-rated movies are a turn-on."**
- **"The sergeant's office because it's illegal."**

- "On the World Trade Center."
- "On our balcony. I like the risk of being seen."
- "On a tennis court."
- "On a pool table."
- "In a museum."
- "In the changing room of a department store."
- "At Yankee Stadium."
- "In a library."
- "On a train."

*Should the Light Be On or Off?*

Our question, "during lovemaking, do you like the light: on, off, or dimmed?" was answered as follows:

| | |
|---|---|
| Dimmed | 84% |
| On | 9% |
| Off | 7% |

At the same time, they told us that in their experience most women like the light off. Maybe you'll change your mind when you read men's reasons for preferring lights dimmed or on.

**The light should be on, or at least dimmed, because being able to see that gorgeous body while you are feeling it sure adds to the excitement.**

I like dimmed lights because I'm not only pleasured by feeling, but derive pleasure from what I see. The visual stimulation is important for me.

I like to see what we're doing. When her breasts are flushed as a result of orgasm, I feel as though we're accomplishing something. And I love to see her facial expressions clearly.

I prefer a dim, romantic glow in the room during lovemaking. I usually have a candle burning. It makes lovemaking feel like something special, which it should always be.

I like making love with the lights on because I love to watch a woman's face while I'm inside her, to see her reactions, and I like positions where I can see what we're doing. Women's bodies are fascinating in dim light, and seeing in her eyes how excited she is makes me feel very sexy.

## CHAPTER NINE

# Attracting a Man Through Your Appearance

This chapter will not only tell you how men like women to look, but will also dispel some of the myths women worry about. The positive advice, and the reassuring way men see us, will certainly help us to be more confident, and worry less about things that are not as important to men as we think. There are requests, though. One was, **"Always be as good-looking as you can."** Another, voiced by a man from Cincinnati, **"Stay attractive—we men know that wrinkles, crow's-feet, and gray hair are inevitable, but women should never get lazy about their looks."**

Fortunately, most requests, as you will see, are not difficult to comply with. If going along with them helps us meet a man, or keep one, why not try it? However, to be always as good-looking as you can means you can *never* be lazy or let go. You may even have to overcome some deep-rooted habits, but let us not overlook here that the results benefit not only the men but us as well. Looking attractive can be an enormous boost to the ego.

I can hear some of you saying, "Looks aren't everything," and you are right, yet sometimes looks are very important. Think of the everlasting first impression. All people have to go on when they meet or see you for the first time is your appearance. It's like a passport, giving vital and revealing information at a glance.

John was a single young executive in his early thirties. His ambitions had left him little time to find a wife or even a steady relationship. However, since the party at Fred's place two weeks ago, the image of a young woman he had seen there kept coming back to him. He could see her lovely figure under the soft fabric that molded her body. Her dark hair fell in curls over her shoulders, and her large, expressive eyes fascinated him. He had to make a conscious effort this morning to concentrate on the meeting with Tom Beech at Onit & Company.

He arrived at the Onit office fifteen minutes early. The receptionist showed him into Beech's office and asked him to wait. A few minutes later a young woman came in; she introduced herself as Mary Olson and asked if he wanted a cup of coffee. Looking up at her, John became confused. When she brought

the coffee, he asked, "Did we meet somewhere before? I have the feeling that I know
you."

Mary laughed. "No, I'm sure we haven't
met before."

As he waited, John observed her. Her figure was hidden by a full skirt and bulky
sweater. Her long dark hair was pulled back
into a pony tail that hung straight down her
back. Her face was young but without any
makeup or expression. John was always annoyed when he couldn't remember things,
and he felt sure that he had seen this girl
somewhere . . . but where? Suddenly it flashed
through his mind: She bore some resemblance
to the girl from the party. But how could that
be? The girl at the party was pretty, this one
was plain. But the resemblance was amazing.
His thoughts were interrupted when Tom
Beech walked into the office.

Later, when John left Onit & Company,
he passed Mary's desk. He stopped and, looking at her again, he asked: "Excuse me, were
you at Fred Winter's party two weeks ago?"

"Yes, I was, how did you know?"

John was surprised and disappointed by
her answer. How could this be the same person? On the way back to his office, he wondered if he'd had a few drinks too many that
night.

Of course, Mary couldn't be expected to
wear the same dress or have quite such

elaborate makeup in the office, but wasn't her appearance when John saw her again too different from before? The special occasion, for which we all make that extra effort—an evening out, a Sunday brunch, a wedding, a dinner dance—are few, and rarely as important as your daily life.

The way we look reflects our character more than we realize. It can say whether we are conservative, outgoing, organized, and clean— or the opposite—and whether we have self-respect and sex appeal. These characteristics are picked up by the world around us, and do affect our relationships with men. Even skeptics have to admit that appearances count—at least for half of what we are, as the following reply confirms:

> **I find that good looks are the combination of subtle things rather than a single thing. Initially it is a question of appearance—the view from across the room, so to speak. Ultimately, however, it is a matter of the mind. The sexiest woman in the world from a physical standpoint will not be sexy if there is no substance to back up the surface.**

## How Important Is Being Beautiful?

Not as important as you may think. It should be noted, though, that being beautiful must not be confused with being attractive. Beauty is a gift of nature, while attractiveness is a goal a woman can always attain, even if she isn't beautiful.

As paradoxical as it sounds, beauty is not always a blessing. It is a well-known fact that extremely beautiful women have sometimes trouble finding dates. They sit home alone many evenings. Why? Because their looks intimidate many men. Regardless of how much they may enjoy looking at a gorgeous woman, being with one often scares them. They also feel that she is more likely to refuse them, and a rejection from her would be more painful and damaging to their ego than from a less beautiful woman.

Question asked in the survey: Which characteristics are important for a long-lasting relationship?

| | |
|---|---|
| Personality | 27% |
| Intelligence | 23% |
| Warmth | 21% |
| Sensuality | 18% |
| Beauty | 9% |
| Submissiveness | 2% |

Here are some reassuring words from the participants:

**A woman with a warm personality can make a man happy for many years.**

It's nice when a woman is good-looking, but a warm personality is definitely more important for a lasting relationship.

Personality and intelligence can overcome anything.

Some men out here care what is behind that pretty face. I have always known that a beautiful body and face are only part of what some—I take that back—most women have to offer. I have found that being with a woman who has intelligence and personality along with those baby blues makes for a much better time.

Personality is the most important factor. After you have made love, there must be something inside her to keep you interested.

As you can see for yourself, beauty is *not* one of the most desired qualities. Personality is!

*Do Men Want Younger Women?*

A question asked in the survey: Do you prefer women who are younger, older, your age, or it doesn't matter?

| | |
|---|---|
| It doesn't matter | 54% |
| Younger | 19% |
| Your age | 16% |
| Older | 11% |

The answers to this question should lay to rest women's preoccupation with their age. They also contradict the common belief that all men want younger women.

The truth is that age doesn't matter. Men don't look at a woman wondering how old she is. They stated over and over that as long as they like what they see, age makes no difference. They further stated that they enjoy and get involved with older women, younger women, and women of their own age. **"Age really doesn't play as big a part as physical well-being. i.e., a woman who watches her weight and figure,"** says a thirty-nine-year-old Ohio engineer.

**"To me age doesn't matter, as long as the woman is still sexy. I've spent time with women ranging from sixteen to thirty-five,"** reports a twenty-one-year-old student from North Dakota. **"Age is not really a factor. I like women who are not younger than twenty, and not older than fifty,"** echoes a twenty-four-year-old computer programmer from Georgia. **"I have really no preference as far as age is concerned. I try not to get involved with women too young (seventeen) or too far into the later years. But I have made love to a lady who was fifty-three, and it was very beautiful,"** wrote in a twenty-five-year-old law student from Texas. **"Age is no barrier. The age syndrome is a myth. Even the prophet Muhammad was married to a woman fifteen**

**years his senior,"** notes a forty-eight-year-old graphic artist from Boston. **"Age is only a factor to those who feel old,"** an Arizona police officer, thirty-one years old, sensibly observed.

The fact that actual age plays so small a role in how we are perceived has a lot to do with the way women take care of themselves today. Women over forty used to be regarded as over the hill. Today we refer to life beginning at forty. Therefore, some of us need to adjust our minds as much as we are trying to adjust our bodies.

My friend Louise had just passed her fifty-fifth birthday when she met Robin, a thirty-seven-year-old tennis pro. Once over the elation of having a younger man paying attention to her, she started to worry. When I asked her what she was worried about, she said, "What do you think people will say? Doesn't it look like I'm trying to make myself look younger? Maybe people think I'm his mother. Is the age difference really not obvious? How long can this last? He will soon find somebody his own age, and where will that leave me?"

I told her that with these doubts in her mind the relationship didn't stand a chance, not now or later. My advice to her was to relax and to enjoy what they shared, and to remember that he was there of his own free will. And if she was still worried about how long they would be together, to remind herself that no couple—regardless of age—ever knows in the beginning how long their relationship will last.

This conversation took place more than six years ago, and I am happy to report that they are still together.

*Which Body Type is Most Exciting?*

When men were asked what body type they found most exciting, their replies indicated that it is not the skinny model type that's admired and envied by most women. A majority of men preferred **"a well-proportioned, firm body, where you can see where the front and back are."**

A schoolteacher from Florida wrote us, **"I like something to hold onto. A round, firm body with nice breasts is what excites me most."** Another man said:

> My favorite body type is medium/slim. I prefer women with curves, a little voluptuous as opposed to the skinny-model bodies I have seen. I also like them fairly muscular, but I do not like fat, by which I mean more than twenty pounds overweight.
>
> Which body type arouses me most? Medium/slim. But voluptuous runs a close second. In other words, I do like a lady

**with a body I can cling to, but a fat body really turns me off.**

**The** *Playboy* **playmate and** *Penthouse* **pet are what I would prefer, because they are voluptuous and that is the sexiest.** (This must be the reason why men prefer *Penthouse* to *Vogue*.)

The actual question asked in the survey was: Which body type arouses you the most?

| | |
|---|---|
| Medium/slim | 55% |
| Voluptuous | 29% |
| Slim/tall | 16% |

As far as women are concerned, there are two messages here:

1. Look at the women in men's magazines and see for yourself that they are not skinny. Therefore, you don't have to worry yourself too much about a few extra pounds.
2. Exercising in order to stay firm is more important than dieting.

To reassure you again on this point, let's hear from a salesman in Orlando: **"A woman's figure can be slightly hefty; the crucial factor is that it be well-proportioned. I prefer**

**women with some meat on them. I don't particularly like the skinny-rail look."**

*What Is the Most Alluring Part of a Woman's Body?*

No, it's not her bust, not her legs, not her buttocks—but her face. We asked in our survey: Which part of a woman's body excites you most?

| | |
|---|---|
| Face | 30% |
| Buttocks | 28% |
| Legs | 22% |
| Bust | 20% |

**"A woman's face excites me more than anything else. The expression tells me what is going on inside, and I love to watch my partner's face when she's nearing orgasm."**

Maybe you're surprised to find out that your face plays the most important role in attracting a man. A thirty-three-year-old dentist gave this rationale:

She has to have a pleasant, interesting face, because that's what I will be looking at 98 percent of the time. I don't even check out the rest of the body if I don't like the face. I have seen extraordinary bodies, but the face negated everything. I really think that the face is the advertising come-on that gets a man to check out the rest.

Another survey question regarding the face was: "Do you like your woman to wear makeup?" A total of 94 percent of the respondents like their women to wear it. How much was another matter. Sixty percent want a little. A married student from the University of Georgia said:

> Enhancement is great, but too much is a big turn-off. Don't fake something that isn't there. College is an incredible place to see some of the most horrible makeup jobs. Some girls look as if their face was a mold; others look as if they got brutally beat up—ugh!

Some other replies:

> A woman's face is the part of her body she uses to advertise. Men love women who wear makeup to enhance such features as cheekbones and eyes. But it shouldn't be put on so heavily that the woman looks like an Indian.

> War paint is unattractive.

> Yes, I love makeup if it's applied properly and isn't overbearing.

What these messages mean is that makeup is a plus so long as it's not too obvious or changes basic facial features. (The biggest outcry is against too heavily applied lipstick; the most appreciated is eye makeup.) This survey showed that the age-old wisdom—a woman can do anything she wants to improve her looks as long as it isn't noticeable—still holds true today.

For those women who wear no makeup at all, these replies might inspire you to see what a little makeup could do for you.

Not forgetting the rest of the body, there are, of course, leg men and breast men out there, too, but they aren't the majority. And for men who do admire breasts most, it's not big ones they're after. **"A woman's breasts excite me most, providing they are neither too large or too small."** It looks as if the Jane Mansfield bosom is no longer a fantasy of today's male.

*How Should You Dress? Sexy? Fashionable? Elegant? or Conservative?*

Conservative styles are a no-no if women want to attract men or please their husbands. Some women believe that because their man dresses conservatively, he likes conservative clothes. What these women don't realize is that this preference applies only to their clothes, not to those of their mate.

We asked in our survey: How do you want

your woman to look when you go out with her?

| | |
|---|---|
| Sexy | 37% |
| Fashionable | 35% |
| Elegant | 21% |
| Conservative | 7% |

**"The way a woman dresses shows me the way she feels about herself and what image she wants to project. A sexy dresser provides immediate stimulation."**

Looking sexy and fashionable are almost of equal importance, but only if a woman is comfortable. **"I love her to look sexy and fashionable, but not if it makes her uncomfortable physically or is embarrassing,"** says a forty-eight-year-old sales director in Minneapolis. The truth is that if you choose your clothes well, even sexy and fashionable styles won't have a negative effect on you.

Fashionable, the second most important look, does not mean the extremes of the latest designs. It does mean wearing clothes that are less than five years old. Our eyes, without our being aware of it (this is as true for men as for women), get used to the latest styles. For example, if narrow-legged pants are in, a wide-legged pair will look terribly passé. And since men react to women mainly by instinct, they associate a dated look with someone who's behind the times—not an appealing characteristic.

Elegant, in third place, is explained this way by a thirty-six-year-old industrial engineer from San Francisco: **"I don't mean fur coats, but something that is classy and appropriate for the occasion. It doesn't matter if the apparel is a year old or brand-new, as long as it conveys an idea of style and elegance."** Another way to explain what elegance stands for comes from a photographer in St. Louis: **"For me an elegant woman is dressed in something that suits her well, and that looks like an outfit, not just any top and skirt or pants."** (The advantage of elegant is that it can be combined with sexy and fashionable anytime.)

An insurance salesman from Massachusetts has yet another viewpoint (shared by over 55 percent of the respondents): **"It's not only important what a woman wears, but how she wears it. Whether it be a T-shirt and jeans, or a black low-cut gown, carrying it off in the right way is what makes her really attractive."**

*What Type of Clothing Attracts*
*a Man or Doesn't?*

Taste is hard to discuss. It varies greatly, and what's right for one woman isn't necessarily suitable for the next. But certain items of clothing men universally find attractive and becoming, and others turn them off just as definitely.

In the eyes of our admirers, the overall silhouette is the most important, and this is influenced by the fit of a garment and how well it is made. Poorly fitting clothes are a turn-off, and so are cheap ones. Simplicity and appropriateness—the right clothes in the right place—are also important. A young woman who thought she looked sexy prompted this comment from a security officer in Toledo: **"I was working in a restaurant which caters mainly to families. One night a young lady walked in wearing a shirt tied below her breasts with a pair of shorts which let half of her rear end show. Usually I would have found this sexy, but in this environment it was no turn-on."** Among the positive items are, in order of preference:

- high-heeled shoes
- low-cut dresses
- miniskirts
- tight jeans
- short shorts (hot pants)
- skirt or dress with slits at the side or front
- halter tops
- tube and tank tops
- silky dresses that move with the body
- lacy or transparent blouses
- bikinis

- ankle bracelets
- any leather garment of good quality

A New England architect of twenty-eight wrote: **"Nothing gets my blood boiling faster than a woman dressed in almost anything made of suede. A tight suede vest and a suede skirt, both partially undone, really turn me on. Leather adds mystery and sensuality to a woman's look."**

Now for the bad news. The following items of clothing or styles are what turns men off most (in order of dislike):

- baggy, loose-fitting clothes of any kind
- long skirts
- full, pleated pants
- baggy pants
- flat shoes and sandals
- bermuda shorts and culottes
- men's style clothing (suits, ties, vests)
- extremely fashionable clothes
- the Valley Girl look
- clothes that are too tight
- sloppy clothes that show an "I don't care" attitude
- bulky clothing (sweaters down to knees)
- dresses or blouses with too many ruffles
- shirts with witty or cutesy sayings

Apart from clothes there is something invisible that enhances a woman and gives her a special aura. We asked in the survey: Does perfume excite or attract you?

Yes   84%
No    16%

**I can't express how much some perfumes excite me.**

**Perfume is always a turn-on.**

**Perfume attracts me a great deal, and later reminds me of her.**

**Very much a turn-on, especially when worn all over the body.**

A thirty-six-year-old heavy-equipment operator from Oregon said it this way: **"Yes, I love perfume on a woman. It attracts me so much that at times I could make love with them just for the way they smell."**

The only word of caution was: **"Perfume should be worn with discretion. Don't use too much or use overpowering scents."**

*With or Without a Bra?*

The question: "When a woman has good breasts, do you prefer her with or without a bra? Why?" did not specify if the woman was their wife, lover, or a date. The replies, however, showed that preferences in this area are strongly influenced by a man's relationship with a woman. "When she is mine, definitely with a bra—when I'm just looking, without." Men who liked bras wrote:

I don't feel that other men should have a clear view of my wife's breasts. Also, a woman with good breasts shows better cleavage and form with a bra.

I'm very possessive.

A bra displays the bosom to greater advantage.

I enjoy seeing cleavage in a low-cut dress.

I enjoy taking a bra off.

A braless woman seems to lack the discipline and mystery which I find attractive.

I don't want her to turn other men on.

They are for me to see and nobody else!

A bra keeps breasts in good condition.

A woman's bra, being an intimate garment, is sexily provocative. But it's the exposed roundness above or between her bra cups that's soooo highly sensuous.

Here are some comments of those who preferred the braless look:

A little tit looks good and never hurts anyone.

I like to see the shape of a woman's nipples, and the idea of her breasts rubbing against the blouse is exciting.

It is nice to see breasts wiggle from side to side.

Nice breasts deserve their freedom.

First of all, it tells me that she is confident about her shape and probably about her sexuality. A woman who choses to go without a bra is generally not displeased that men find her attractive, and to me this is a low-key sexual signal that she enjoys being a woman, which allows me to put aside that little voice in the back of my head telling me that I'm a male chauvinist. Finally, I like the braless look because it usually gets me hard.

A woman without a bra shows self-confidence, is inviting, wild, and adventurous.

It's nice to see nipples poking through her clothing, and I really get turned on if the areola shows through. Medium to large nipples are the biggest turn-on for me.

Good breasts to me mean firm or fairly firm (a little sag is only natural). So if a woman's breasts are up there where they belong, she looks great without a bra because she looks free, easy, and comfortable with herself.

Apart from these there is a third possibility, one that pleases all men:

I like her to wear a bra in public, but when we are at home I like her to wear as little as possible.

A bra helps to keep my mind off sex, but when we are alone and she is braless, I can't take my eyes off her.

It's like she's saying her breasts are accessible to me.

*Can Shoes Help You Catch His Eye?*
The most effective way to look feminine and sexy is to wear high-heeled shoes. (Alas, if only someone could combine comfort with spike heels.) A question in our survey asked: Does it increase your excitement when a woman wears high-heeled shoes?

| Yes | 80% |
|-----|-----|
| No  | 20% |

During lovemaking?

| No  | 52% |
|-----|-----|
| Yes | 48% |

High heels make legs appear longer and curvier. They also add height and give a woman's silhouette a slimmer look. No man ever misses a pair of legs with high-heeled shoes. The style of the shoes doesn't matter, it's the heel that counts. A thirty-seven-year-old insurance agent from New York commented, **"High-heeled sandals with a lady's manicured toes exposed drive me crazy."** Another said: **"High heels lead the eye up the leg and flatter the silhouette of a woman."**

**"Boots with high heels are also a turn-on. They convey sensuality and with a pair of pants tucked into them, they look especially attractive and sporty."**

Here, combined with advice, a word of warning from a man in Dayton, Ohio: **"I am extremely turned off by women who wear flat shoes, because I feel that a high-heeled shoe is the trademark of a vibrant, sexy woman."**

As we see, high heels not only have their effect on the street, but can also be helpful in bed. Almost half the respondents agreed that it added to the excitement of making love. "**Even when a woman is naked, I like her to wear high-heeled shoes.**" A doctor in Cleveland, stated, "**Whenever a woman wears her high-heeled shoes to bed, it always increases the pleasure.**"

*Are Glasses Seen as Unattractive?*

Women who have to wear glasses often feel cheated by Mother Nature. But in answer to the question, "Do you find women wearing glasses less attractive?" eighty-four percent of these surveyed answered in the negative. A twenty-nine-year-old free-lance writer in New York wrote:

> **Emphatically no. On the contrary, many women's beauty is enhanced by a nice pair of stylish glasses. They can decorate a face, because large lenses may serve as display windows for a fascinating pair of eyes. Glasses can also suggest an additional dimension to a lady's personality, i.e., intelligence, thoughtfulness, etc.**

Others said:

> **Glasses can make a woman look better, providing they are the right style.**

> **On the contrary, some women look beautiful with glasses.**

If they are fashionable and not horn-rimmed, glasses can be very sexy when they are the right ones.

For some men, like this twenty-five-year-old clerk typist in the Army, spectacles can even hold a hidden promise: "In no way do I find women wearing glasses less attractive. As a matter of fact, it looks sexy, especially combined with a bikini, because, with almost everything else uncovered, the glasses are hiding eyes that could be looking my way."

*Are Long Fingernails a Turn-On?*

Most women would love to have long nails, regardless of what men want. And since we see our hands more than anyone else does, having pretty hands and nails means pleasing ourselves first. But what do men want? Question asked in the survey: Do long fingernails turn you on?

| | |
|---|---|
| Yes | 53% |
| No | 47% |

This was one of the few questions in which the answers split nearly evenly. Even the men who find long nails a plus have reservations, such as:

I like long nails, but not too long.

**Long fingernails turn me on, but they must not be too long.**

**Yes, long fingernails are exciting if they are real, not when they are sculptured or artificial.**

The mistake often made when nails are sculptured, and the reason why men detect it, is that they are made too long, which gives them an unnatural look. This brings us to the question of what looks unnatural or too long:

- "Anything that interferes with doing things naturally."
- "Anything that looks like claws is unattractive."
- "The right length is when the nail extends about quarter of an inch over the fingertip."
- "I like medium length, clean, and natural-looking."

And then some men still agree with the old-fashioned idea that long nails "tell me that the woman probably doesn't want to work."

Almost in total agreement were the replies on the following two points:

1. Hands and nails well manicured, well taken care of, are a must. After all,

who wants to be touched (and we are talking not only about handshakes here) by a hand that is not soft or pleasing?

2. Almost every man in our survey said that he likes nails to be polished. The majority prefer a light, pretty color; the rest like bright red, which they find exciting because **"it activates the imagination for things to come."**

## CHAPTER TEN

# Seducing a Man Through Your Behavior

Now that you've caught his eye through your appearance, you have him halfway in your net. To close the net and pull it out of the water, you have to use your feminine charm.

As we have seen, no man wants a submissive, helpless, or coy woman. Most women out there don't fit that description, but it is mentioned here just in case some women think they have to pretend to be something they are not. As we have heard over and over, what men want today is an assertive woman, yet one who is feminine and sexy.

**"I like women who aren't afraid to take charge, and don't wait for me to make all the moves. Assertive women are the most stimulating,"** feels an intern in San Diego.

Assertive, not aggressive! Some people get these two concepts mixed up, and for many people they are even the same. During radio interviews I have done with regard to this survey, the interviewers asked: "So you found out that men like aggressive women?"

After clarifying this point many times, and not only for radio interviewers, I have become sensitive to the negative connotations the word "assertive" has. *Assertive means getting what you want in a nonaggressive way.* With most people, anywhere in the world, using your charm and standing steadfastly for what you believe in will get you anything you want.

*Is Sexual Experience Important?*

It certainly is! **"With sex, as with other things in life, experience is a plus. Sharing something with a knowledgeable person lessens the responsibility; it allows us to learn something, and it prevents us from losing time by learning or teaching."**

This is the feeling of the majority of men; the time when everyone wanted a virgin seems to have passed. Following are the answers to the question asked in the survey: Do you prefer to make love to a woman who is:

| | |
|---|---|
| Sexually experienced | 86% |
| Sexually inexperienced | 11% |
| A virgin | 3% |

As you can see, nobody wants a virgin. (Unfortunately, no one explained how one overcomes this dilemma). **"A virgin is extremely hard to loosen up, and a sexually inexperienced woman is uninteresting."** But they did give us their reasons for wanting an experienced woman to make love with:

**Sexually experienced women are more enjoyable because they have been around a man's body long enough not to be afraid of it.**

**I prefer a woman who knows what feels good to a man.**

**Because I know that mutual pleasures can be shared.**

**From a sexually experienced woman one can always learn something.**

**An experienced woman is open, creative, and sensitive to her and my needs.**

**She can bring something with her to make our lovemaking mutually enjoyable, instead of a teacher-pupil session.**

*Don't Take a First Date Too Seriously*
Look at it as fun, as an adventure, as something that might turn out to be an exciting experience—but then again, it might not. To avoid disappointment, go on a first date with

a wait-and-see attitude. Feel confident, not anxious. Don't worry if he likes you or not. The real question is do *you* find *him* as nice, or nicer, as when you accepted his invitation. Is he really what you expected?

A wait-and-see approach allows you to stay objective, which is extremely important in the beginning. You won't be so ready to rationalize liking someone or feeling lucky that he asked you out. Even if you haven't had a date in the past few months, it's no reason to feel lucky or compromise. If he doesn't turn out to be what you need and want, keep looking. More men are out there than you know.

On the other hand, there are men about whom it is difficult to come to a decision on a first impression or date. They are usually the quiet type, not outgoing, not exciting at first, but reassuring. When you meet one of them and you're uncertain if you like him, by all means do find out before saying no.

Diane is thirty-eight, divorced, with a six-year-old child. During a business trip she met a quiet, pleasant man who also lives in Chicago. He asked her if he could call her once they were back home. "Why not?" was her reply, forgetting about him immediately. Two weeks later he called and they agreed to go to the theater. When the day arrived, Diane had changed her mind. She didn't want to go out with him anymore. He was too quiet for her, too shy, and not very interesting or challenging. She asked her mother, who was baby-sitting for her son, to tell him that she couldn't make it.

Fortunately for Diane, her mother was a wise woman. She said, "There is no way I will excuse you, and furthermore, I don't think you should sit here at home alone. Why don't you give the man a chance? He might be nicer and more interesting than he appears." Not because Diane agreed with her mother, but rather to please her, she went out that night.

More than nine years later, his interesting personality, which was not apparent at first, has kept this relationship alive and well.

*Make a Pass at Him if He Doesn't*

This survey showed how painfully shy many men are around women. These men need more than encouragment, they need you to make the first step. Therefore, if you see a man you like and really want to know him—if you think he is worth going after—you have to take charge of the situation and approach him. Find a reason or excuse to talk to him. A question or a request for help might be enough to get things rolling. All that's really needed is to break the ice, and he'll take it from there. To encourage you to take this first step, here are the testimonies of two men who feel that they have missed a lot because of women's hesitation to go after what they want.

The first one is from a businessman, forty-eight, in Orlando:

> I think most men get tired of doing the chasing. Now I'm married, but when I was single I remember how frustrating it was to go out for the evening and come home alone. I've often wondered how many women have said, "Boy, he's cute" or "I'd sure like to go out with him," but never did because they were waiting for the man to make the first move. I know that we have women's lib now, but it's still not very evident on the bar scene.
>
> I also know there are still some macho men who want to be in charge, but I've talked to lots of men in my life, and most of them would love a woman to come on to them. Why do you think men still pay for sex?

The second comment is from a telephone repair man, twenty-nine, in South Bend: "Women should be more open about their attraction to men. I've often found myself in situations where I thought a woman didn't

even notice me, only to find out later that this woman indeed found me attractive."
And others said:

Don't be shy, understand that the guy on the other side of the room who is looking at you might want you as much as you want him.

Some men are shy. If you are attracted to him, let him know. Don't be afraid of what people might say. Anything can be yours if you want it, in relationships as well as in other aspects of life.

I like when a woman makes a pass at me. I am somewhat shy and therefore could miss the opportunity.

I enjoy being pursued, it makes the relationship more equal.

It excites me to know somebody wants me enough to take a chance of rejection.

It makes me realize she likes what she sees—a complete satisfaction.

Remember these words the next time you see someone you want. Don't let him slip away without having tried.

*Treat Men as Sex Objects—Tell Them When You Want to Make Love to Them*

Most women feel that being taken as a sex object is nothing but an insult, whereas many men would love to be seen that way. They find it complimentary and stimulating because, as this stockbroker from Miami tells us, **"Men like to be regarded as sex objects. It makes them feel needed."**

And this doctor from Connecticut said: **"Don't tell your man only that you love him, tell him also that you enjoy his body sexually. Most men like to be thought of as sex objects. We like women who crave our bodies, it's exciting."**

Maybe the reason men react so differently is that the experience is rare for them. Or maybe they feel that being a sex object does not diminish any of their other qualities. From the reasons they give us here we will find out why they would welcome it:

**I like being the sex object for a change.**

**It takes a lot of pressure off me.**

**It gives you a good feeling inside.**

**I don't have to be responsible, and I know I will be making love with, rather than to, a woman.**

I find it exciting because I'm an average guy and it's a great boost to my ego.

It would be a different experience.

It's something new to me and would relieve my mind of the tension and fear of rejection. It also opens up new channels of communication.

I love women who like to make love as much as I do.

It's very complimentary, it shows she finds me attractive.

It's nice to be picked up.

I like to be hunted, it means she really likes me.

Sign of control, she knows a good man when she sees one.

Nothing beats the feeling of being desired.

This knowledge gives women a chance to turn the tables, to look at men also as a way of sexual pleasure and fulfillment. And we can go even a step further. If we meet a man who attracts us physically, we can feel free to tell him so. How can we be so sure? By looking at the replies to the survey question: Do you like it when a woman asks you to go to bed with her?

**"Yes, I like to be seduced"** was the answer of 99 percent of the men. (The chances of your meeting a man in the other 1% are very slim.)

The second part of the question: Does it excite you? Why? produced reasons like these:

It's exciting because it's flattering.

Any woman who wants it enough to ask beats a million who sit back.

I like a woman who doesn't play games. If she wants to make love, she shouldn't necessarily wait for me to ask her. Women who love sex and don't use it as a stepping stone to something else—marriage, money, position—are infinitely more exciting than women who sidestep, tease, and use sex as bait.

It is a great way for a woman to let you know how much she likes you.

Because I know that she's turned on by me and only me at that moment, and it gets me hot.

Because I'm painfully shy.

It makes me perform better and I feel real good about myself.

It excites me, both sexually and otherwise, and it makes for a more solid and lasting relationship.

The third part of the question was: How should she say it?

| | |
|---|---|
| Directly | 61% |
| Either way | 24% |
| Indirectly | 15% |

I like a woman to ask me directly to go to bed with her. It excites me because I'm an extremely passive person.

Yes, directly, because I believe it indicates a certain level of self-confidence on her part, and she will probably be more adventurous and responsive in bed.

Should be said directly. It does excite me because I know she desires me, and won't make love to me because she thinks she should.

A statement like that reaffirms my ego and my attractiveness.

Yes, I like when a woman asks me to go to bed with her. She should say it directly, mostly because I have to be, like many men, hit over the head to realize that a woman wants to sleep with me. It excites me because it's a boost to my ego.

If you still feel hesitant about being direct for fear of embarrassment or rejection, remember these words, which came from an attorney in Baltimore: **"It's an honor to be asked."**

Others said:

Making the first move doesn't mean prowling the streets, but it does mean that women can and should do the asking. I have such a fantastic wife and sex life today, partly because on our first date, when it was clear that we were taken with each other, she said, "When we go out next week, would you make love to me please?" And this is a classy and educated lady.

I like it because she as a woman has chosen me, among all others, as the man she most wants to be with. Such forthright honesty is totally refreshing and absolutely provocative!

When a woman says that she wants me directly, we don't get our signals crossed.

**Yes, it excites me because the anticipation of making love is intensified. When a woman says, "Let's go to bed," you know she has certain things in mind, and I can't wait to find out what's in store for me.**

### Setting the Tone of a Relationship

How successful we are in a relationship is often determined by how we start it. If you accept disagreeable behavior in the beginning, it will be hard, if not impossible, to change it later without being labeled a nag or worse. If you miss the right moment to tell a man who you are and how you expect to be treated, you can lose the chance for his respect forever.

Sue, a twenty-four-year-old secretary, met Gary, who is twenty-eight, two months ago. They have been going out since then, and she likes him very much. What she doesn't like is that Gary asks her to call him at a certain time to set up their next date. On a recent Saturday afternoon he wasn't home for her call, nor did he phone her. The result was a solitary evening. She was quite upset when she told me about it. When I advised Sue to tell Gary honestly that she doesn't always want to be the one to call him and that she was annoyed when he spoiled her Saturday evening, her response was: "Oh, I can't do that. It's not my nature to tell people off, I'm too polite."

Sue's reasoning had nothing to do with politeness. She's afraid of losing Gary if she speaks up. Her lack of courage is setting her up for her next disappointment. Since she didn't object to his thoughtlessness this time, nothing will prevent him from acting the same way again. Giving Gary the benefit of the doubt, he may not have acted out of malice, but simply concluded that it made no difference to Sue.

If situations like this do finally bring on complaints from people like Sue, men like Gary reply: "But why didn't you ever tell me you didn't like it?" (Remember earlier testimonies: **"We are not mind readers!"**) And to add insult to injury, the fault now seems to lie with the woman!

Another pitfall to avoid in the beginning is to be overzealous. Don't offer to cook dinner for him on your first date. This is the time for him to spoil you. Besides, at this stage of the game, he's more interested in impressing you than in sampling your cooking. Offering to cook for him a little later will get you more appreciation than on the first date. The way to a man's heart may be through his stomach, but not right away!

*Don't Scare Him with Your Independence*

It's indeed wonderful that women no longer need to find husbands to support them. They are capable of standing on their own two feet. It's a victory no woman should ever stop rejoicing in, but let's do it in private, among ourselves. Don't use independence as a weapon, as a way of telling men that we don't need them anymore. Most men are well aware of our freedom and are happy for us, but it hasn't made them lose sight of other important things. A twenty-two-year-old medical assistant in the Army summarized it this way: **"Equal rights are great, but so are nice legs."**

Nor should we think that our independence has changed all the rules of the mating game. It hasn't. When a man invites a woman for dinner, she doesn't have to say: "Yes, but let's go dutch." Does she think he can't pay for it? That would be an insult. Or is her need to demonstrate her self-reliance so great that she can't gracefully accept a dinner invitation? You may argue that you don't want to owe a man anything, but be objective for a moment: What could you possibly owe him for a dinner? You're spending your time with him, you're both having a pleasant evening—isn't that enough? If in his mind it isn't, that's his problem, not yours. Or maybe you don't find it fair that men always have to pay? In that case invite him out on special occasions like his birthday, a promotion, or an anniversary. He will be delighted and you won't feel that the world is unfair. After you have developed a solid relationship with him, the two of you can find a financial arrangement that makes both of you comfortable.

Another area in which women have become very forward and free is in their physical approach. This brings to mind a story a twenty-eight-year-old schoolteacher from Rhode Island wrote us:

> The last time I went to a discotheque, I admired a beautiful blond girl who was standing at the other side of the bar. I finally caught her eye and smiled at her, hoping that she would smile back. Well, her reaction was totally unexpected. She walked over to me, said, "Hi, there," and kissed me on both cheeks. Of course, I would be lying if I said I wasn't pleased that she came over, but her readiness did take away from the prickling excitement and the suspense I always feel when I'm not sure if a woman is willing or not.

## Don't Assume Sex Is All He Wants

From what we read and hear about sex, you can get the impression that sex is *all* a man wants. But is it? No, not on the first date, and not even later.

> Be more responsive to those of us who aren't just out there for a one-night stand every day of the week. I'm basically trying to get to know you better because I think I might enjoy your company, not because I want to get it on before I know what your first name is. It all comes down to trusting a little bit more.

**Slow down a little. By not giving yourself or me a chance to find out what we are all about, you may miss something real.**

There is certainly some truth to the notion that courting is based on primitive feelings, and that having sex with you is on his mind, but it doesn't have to happen the first time you go out with him. (I know exceptions to what I just said, but in this book we are interested in the majority, not the exceptions.)

**"If a woman is not compassionate and caring, if all a man wants is sex, he can find a hooker and have a sure thing, instead of wining and dining a woman"** is the opinion of many men on this point.

A man who takes you out is as curious about you as you are about him. He wants to find out who you are, what you are all about, what the two of you might have in common. But most of all he wants to know how much you like him. The best way to show him, and to find out what you want to know, is to make him talk about himself—his work (this subject never fails), where he grew up, and what his interests are. Your interest in him will put him at ease, and he will open up to you. He will feel that you understand and like him, that you care. This can be the foundation of a happy relationship.

## CHAPTER ELEVEN

# Survey-ing Your Man

The preceding testimonies on how to please a man are the result of the thoughts, feelings, desires, and fantasies of thousands of American men. Yet regardless of the similarities —and there are many—every man is still an individual, just a little bit different from the next guy.

Now that you are aware of all the ground rules, the time has come to find out what makes your own man similar or different from the rest. To help you do so, this chapter gives you the questionnaire the survey participants completed. Ask your man to fill it out. When he gives it back to you, read it alone and be prepared for some surprises. Whatever you find out, don't take it as a criticism of yourself, but look at it as the first step to a better communication. That's what this woman from Houston, Texas did: **"Here are the answers to my husband's self-examina-**

tion. Some of the answers upset me a little, but I found out many things about him I didn't know. If nothing else, it helped me in shopping for my clothes. Thank you very much."

And here is a lady from California:

Thank you for your questionnaire. I thought it was great! My husband and I decided that I'd ask the questions and write them down for him. He loved the idea and so did I because I got to hear all these answers—some of the things I had never thought of before or asked him about, including little things like "He doesn't like the nail polish I wear every day." With regard to our sex life the answers were very stimulating to both of us.

## Questionnaire

1. How can you tell if a woman is sexy? By the way she:
   Dresses
   Behaves
   Moves
   Talks

2. Which part of a woman's body excites you most?
    Face
    Bust
    Legs
    Buttocks
    Other

3. Which body type arouses you the most?
    Slim/tall
    Medium/slim
    Voluptuous
    Other

4. Which characteristic stimulates you the most?
    Assertiveness
    Shyness
    Helplessness
    Vulgarity

5. Do you prefer to make love to a woman who is:
    Sexually experienced
    Sexually inexperienced
    A virgin

6. Do you prefer women who are:
    Younger
    Older
    Your age
    It doesn't matter

7. Name an actress whom you find very sexy and tell us why.

   _____

   _____

8. How do you want your woman to look when you go out with her (you may check more than one)?

      Elegant
      Sexy
      Conservative
      Fashionable
      Other

9. Do you like your woman to wear makeup?

      Yes
      No
      A little
      To wear nail polish?
      Yes
      No
      A little

10. Do long fingernails turn you on?

      Yes
      No

11. Does perfume excite you or attract you?

      Yes
      No

12. Do you find women wearing glasses less attractive?
    Yes
    No

13. Which characteristics are important for a long-lasting relationship (you may check more than one)?
    Beauty
    Sensuality
    Intelligence
    Assertiveness
    Submissiveness
    Personality
    Warmth

14. When a woman has good breasts, do you prefer her with _____ or without a bra? _____

    Why?_____

15. Which kind of underwear excites you?
    Tastefully sexy
    Naughty and provocative
    Garter belts and stockings
    Panty hose
    No underwear
    Name the item (e.g., a G-string panty) that turns you on the most:_____
    What type or types of underwear turn you off (please list)?_____

16. Which color do you find most provocative and sexy in underwear?_____

17. What type of sleepwear do you find arousing?
    Long nightgowns
    Short nightgowns
    Transparent nightgowns
    Pajamas

18. Besides sexy underwear and sleepwear, what clothing items (e.g., boots, or low-cut dresses) excites you (please list)?

    _____

    What type of clothing turns you off (e.g. flat shoes)?

    _____

19. Does it increase your excitement when a woman wears high-heeled, sexy shoes?
    Yes
    No
    During lovemaking:
    Yes
    No

20. Do you like it when a woman asks you to go to bed with her?
    Yes
    No
    How should she say it?
    Directly

Indirectly
Does it excite you?
Yes
No
Why?_____

21. Do you like it when a woman runs her fingers through your hair and over your chest?
Yes
No

22. Do you want a woman to be completely naked during lovemaking?
Yes
No
Or wearing something, such as a garter belt (please list)?

_____

23. Do you like to undress a woman?
Yes
No
How?
During foreplay
Everything at once
Partially
Or do you prefer that she undresses herself:
In front of you
In privacy

24. Do you like to be undressed by a woman?
    Yes
    No
    Why not?_____
    Shirt and tie only
    Completely

25. During lovemaking, do you like the light:
    On
    Off
    Dimmed

26. Besides the bedroom, what is your favorite place(s) to make love (please list)?____
    Why do you prefer this place(s)?_____

27. While making love, should a woman be:
    Aggressive
    Suggestive
    Initiatory
    Clinging
    Shy

28. Does it excite you when a woman asks you to touch her?
    Yes
    No

29. Do you like a woman to give you a massage?
    Yes
    No
    Where?_____

30. What kind of remarks will make you feel more aroused?

   _____

31. Does pornographic language:
   Shock you
   Excite you
   Make no difference

32. Do you like to take a bath or shower with your partner?
   Yes
   No
   Why?_____

33. After lovemaking, what should a woman do to arouse you again?_____

34. After a night of passion, do you like to:
   Be served breakfast in bed
   Make breakfast with her
   Prepare breakfast for her

35. Would you like your partner to be sexually more:
   Responsive
   Initiatory
   Adventurous
   Assertive

36. In conversations, what subjects or remarks before, during, and/or after turn you off?
_____
_____
_____


37. For married men only

How long have you been married? ___

Are you sexually attracted to other women?

    Sometimes    Why?_____

    Often    Why?_____

    Never    Why?_____

Is your sex life:

  Routine

  Satisfactory

  Very good

  Exciting

  Not enough

What do you think your woman could improve on (you may check more than one)? Her:

    Clothes

    Hair

    Makeup

    Manicure

    Figure

Would you mind if she spent more money on the above?

    Yes

    No

38. If you had to give one suggestion to women regarding how to be better lovers, what would it be?